YOU THINK YOU KNOW ME

THE TRUE STORY OF HERB BAUMEISTER AND THE HORROR AT FOX HOLLOW FARM

RYAN GREEN

For Helen, Harvey, Frankie and Dougie

Disclaimer

This book is about real people committing real crimes. The story has been constructed by facts but some of the scenes, dialogue and characters have been fictionalised.

Polite Note to the Reader

This book is written in British English except where fidelity to other languages or accents are appropriate. Some words and phrases may differ from US English.

Copyright © Ryan Green 2018

All rights reserved

ISBN-13: 978-1987520668
ISBN-10: 1987520661

YOUR FREE BOOK IS WAITING

From bestselling author Ryan Green

There is a man who is officially classed as **"Britain's most dangerous prisoner"**

The man's name is Robert Maudsley, and his crimes earned him the nickname **"Hannibal the Cannibal"**

This free book is an exploration of his story...

★★★★★ *"Ryan brings the horrifying details to life. I can't wait to read more by this author!"*

Get a free copy of **Robert Maudsley: Hannibal the Cannibal** when you sign up to join my Reader's Group.

www.ryangreenbooks.com/free-book

CONTENTS

Introduction 7
Getting Weird 13
Adrift 20
Original Prankster 27
The Good Years 40
The I-70 Strangler 44
Lonely Summer 53
The Summer of Love 63
Downward Spiral 78
The Investigation 86
Descent into Chaos 101
Loose Ends 108
Conclusion 112
Want More? 116
Every Review Helps 117
About Ryan Green 118
More Books by Ryan Green 119
Free True Crime Audiobook 123

Introduction

You don't get to grow up as a gay man in Indiana without learning to read people. When you live in a world where a wink or a sly joke at the wrong time can end with you getting beaten in the streets, you either shut down completely or you start to learn the secret code that lets you identify other people like you out in the wild. The words that people say, even the tone that they use, those things can be lies, but the way that they carry themselves and the way they look at you—it takes a real piece of work to fake those.

Even in gay bars like the 501 Club, the sacred safe spaces of the community where it was meant to be alright to relax and be yourself without having to worry about the consequences, there were men who just didn't fit. Men who shouldn't be there. The criminals out looking for somebody to roll for pocket change. The married men who couldn't let the straight veneer fall off until they were eight drinks in and halfway to unconscious. To start with, that is what Tony thought that he was looking at.

The guy wasn't dressed up. He wasn't in clothes flamboyant enough to border on drag, or even wearing any of those little hints that he was into men, but most of the guys here came straight from work and didn't have a chance to gussy up, so that didn't prove anything in itself. His clothes weren't terribly flattering, but the stereotype that gay men were all obsessed with fashion needed to go and die in a ditch somewhere anyway. You just had to look at the mess of silk t-shirts, Hawaiian shirts, and patterned skirts in this bar to realise straight people didn't have the monopoly on tasteless clothing. His eyes were darting around all over the place the whole time that Tony was watching him cross the room. That wasn't a big warning sign either; there was a lot to see in a place like this. Lots of bright colours and flashing lights, not to mention the tantalising hint of bare skin out on the dance floor. Even if there were chemically induced reasons for the guy's overactive eyeballs, nobody here was going to judge. Half of the room had probably taken a line of coke in the bathroom at some point or another. That was just the scene.

If he had just looked uptight, then everyone probably would have just written him off as another married man going off cruising for something a bit more interesting, but that was almost the opposite of the problem. The guy was so loose that when he sloped onto a bar stool, it wouldn't have surprised Tony if he just slithered right off and into a puddle on the floor. He seemed completely boneless. So comfortable that he had come out the other side into some other weird territory. Maybe he was on something stronger than coke, floating through the bar on one of the old hippies' mind-expanding trips. It wouldn't be the first time. Hell, it could be a real magical adventure at this time of night between the strobing lights and the pretty young things. This guy didn't seem to notice anyone or anything—he was almost startled when he hit the bar. Most of the bodies by the bar were clamouring for attention, one way or another. They wanted a drink, or they wanted to be seen, viewed from afar and admired. This guy... he just stood and stared straight ahead. Not a good plan if you ever want to get served. The bartenders here were pretty fair, as well as being more than a little cute, and they tried to serve folks based on who got there first, but even they wouldn't remember somebody who wasn't even trying to make eye contact.

Tony stared at him for a little while. Just taking in the whole picture. The still life of some stoned-out-of-his-gourd weirdo lurking in a gay bar, staring at a wall. He was tall, almost lanky, and while the bar was filled with constant chatter he was so silent it was deafening. Tony had seen him before. He was a regular on the scene, always lurking in the background, always slightly out of focus. Tony couldn't place exactly where he had seen him or when, but the face was familiar. There weren't so many available men in Indianapolis for even someone as unobtrusive as this to go completely unnoticed. When Tony's eyes had worked their way back up the familiar stranger's body to his face, he froze. The eyes had stopped darting around now. They were locked in place and burning with passion. Tony sidled closer, ever so carefully, to see what the guy was staring at. His stomach dropped when he saw the poster taped to the mirror behind the bar. It was a missing poster, and he'd had to beg the bartender to get it up there himself.

Roger Goodlet was another regular on the scene, a good friend of Tony's, even if they had never made it anything more. He liked to drink and he liked to party, and that meant that when he vanished without a trace, the police didn't do much more than shrug. Families were a touchy subject for men like Roger, but his parents seemed to be more upset than relieved when he vanished, so Tony had gotten in touch and offered to help however he could. Roger's case had been passed around a bit within the police department in the first month, but his parents had gotten tired of waiting. They had hired some private investigator and run off these posters, and since the last time anybody could remember seeing Roger was in a gay bar, that was where Tony had gone out and plastered his posters. The good people of Indianapolis couldn't give a damn if a gay man vanished. Most of them would have considered it a net gain for the city. But here amongst his own people, Tony had hoped that someone—anyone—would care enough to at least call the damned detective. If it had been the police, he could understand their reluctance, but a private eye? Not one of them had called. Not one of them even seemed to remember Roger now that he was gone. It wasn't just like he had vanished, it was like he had never existed. The scene survived on a constant diet of fresh faces and young bodies. Roger and even Tony were a little bit invisible, but it still stung that they could be forgotten so easily, so eagerly, by the people who were meant to give a damn.

Except that this weirdo with his business casual suit and his coked-up mannerisms was giving a damn. He was mesmerised, staring at the black and white photocopy of the one good picture of an adult Roger that his parents had been able to find. If Tony hadn't been curious about this not-quite-a-stranger before, then that stare would have been enough to pique his interest. This close, he could see the intensity on the guy's face. He could see the tip of his tongue flitting out to wet his lips. Realisation settled into the pit of Tony's stomach like a lead weight. He didn't know why, but he felt certain in his gut that this not-stranger had been the one to take Roger. That he had taken him and maybe even killed him. He didn't know where that knowledge was coming from. He didn't know what it was about the hungry look on this guy's face that made him so damned certain that he had killed Roger. But he knew.

He was already frozen, already stalled in his stealthy approach along the bar. Fear had shot a ramrod right up his spine. He couldn't prove it, but he knew that he was standing just a few feet away from a killer. The guy couldn't look away from the poster, and that was the only thing that was keeping Tony safe in this moment. This guy's sick fixation. The certainty passed almost as quickly as the fear. This was a safe place after all. The kind of place where Tony could let his guard down once or twice a week without having to worry about violence. There was no reason to be afraid. Not here. Just like there had been no reason for Roger to be afraid. Tony's feet were moving without his input. Dragging him closer and closer to the killer. A gut feeling and a nervous episode were not evidence. He couldn't go running to the cops, or even the infinitely more sympathetic private investigator. Not with a funny look on the face of some guy who might be high out of his mind. It just wasn't enough. This guy might just be another one of the invisible people on the scene and Tony might just be losing his mind worrying about a friend who really might have just taken a trip to Vegas without telling anybody.

The problem with that realisation was that his feet were still propelling him forward. One way or the other, he had to know. If he walked away right now he would spend the rest of his life wondering if that gut reaction had been right. If this man from the background of so many of his precious memories was the one that he had been looking for all this time. He had to take this as far as he could take it. His treacherous feet had him almost close enough to touch the guy. Close enough to smell his mall-rat cologne and see the patchy stubble where he hadn't shaved properly. Tony's plan was only just taking shape when the guy realised he was there. Tony drank in the details of the guy's face as he turned. He was a bit older than Tony might have picked for himself. His looks were really nothing to write home about, but he had a wry little smile that made Tony think that he might be funny. That smile had a promise that he might even be a good time.

You don't get to grow up to be a gay man in Indiana without having some guts. Tony wasn't one of the men who slunk in here with his collar turned up and an eye always open in case he was recognised. This was his life. He didn't run around behind some poor woman's back pretending that he wanted her, that he loved her, just because that would be the easy thing to do. Courage takes many forms, and on that night, for Tony, it took the form of a smirk.

'Can I buy you a drink, stranger?'

The man's distant gaze flickered for a moment, then a mask of normalcy slipped over his features. Suddenly he looked just like everyone else. No wonder he was so damned forgettable when he could just slip into a hollowed-out persona at will. He smiled at Tony and held out a hand to shake. Business-casual mannerisms to go with the suit. 'Hey there. Brian Smart, nice to meet you.'

Tony was watching for it, so he saw the corner of Brian's mouth twinge as he said the fake name. Brian Smart. Brian Smart. Jesus. It was like a toddler's idea of a fake name. So obvious you couldn't even believe it was a fake.

Tony took his hand, and Brian's fingers trailed up to encircle his wrist. 'What is a pretty young thing like you doing in a place like this?'

Tony played up his embarrassment at the pathetic attempt at flirtation and studied Brian's face for another long moment. Even if he was wrong, that little smile had some potential. This guy wasn't too hard on the eyes. He could get through this. If it meant being able to shake off the sense of doom that had been following him around since Roger had vanished, then Tony would probably put up with a lot worse than some tepid sex with a firmly average looking guy. If it went the other way and Brian turned out to be the monster that Tony suspected, then he wouldn't be taken by surprise like some of the more vulnerable kids in the bar. He was prepared. He swallowed his fear, he swallowed his pride, and he broadened his smile at Brian.

'How about that drink?'

Getting Weird

Herb Baumeister was born in April of 1947, the first, but not last, child of successful anaesthesiologist Herbert Baumeister, Senior, and his loving wife, Elizabeth. His first few years were spent in the Butler-Tarkington neighbourhood of Indiana, then his siblings were born, one after the other: a sister, Barbara, a brother, Brad, and another brother, Richard, nine years after Herb himself was born. With the house becoming increasingly cramped and Herbert Senior's continuing success in his medical practice, the family relocated to the affluent Washington Township, just north of Indianapolis. Herb was delighted by the move. He had spent his childhood doting on his younger siblings, joyfully indulging all of their flights of fancy, and now they had far more space to run around in. Herb was a perpetual practical joker, able to draw laughter out of his siblings and his parents no matter how dark their moods. He was a caring, sensitive boy, beloved by his mother and treated fairly by his often-absent father. As the eldest child, he was the only one to truly remember what their first home had been like. While the rest grew up accustomed to luxury as standard, he knew that a life like this could only be acquired through diligence, hard work, and even a little bit of brilliance. Herb did well in school. He had a close circle of friends and seemed to be popular among his peer group. His parents were wealthy, but he seemed to have inherited the entrepreneurial spirit that would likely make him pursue and find success of his own. In short, Herb Baumeister looked like he was going to live a charmed life. Then puberty hit.

There are many mental illnesses that first manifest with the onset of puberty. Brain chemistry that functions perfectly one day may brutally misfire when exposed to a sudden rush of hormones. The change in Herb wasn't as sudden as it is for some people. His personality and the way that he interacted with the world around him remained the same from one day to the next, but the passions that drove him, the subjects that interested him, and the extremes to which he would take his practical jokes just kept on twisting. He started to care less about the laughter of the other children and more about amusing himself. He turned inwards and set about satisfying some of the new impulses that he was developing.

The culture of his school was focused primarily on sports, so the more bookish Herb never quite fitted in with the popular crowd. He had accepted quite early on that he was never going to blend in with the school's general population, so he strove instead to stand out. He never dated throughout his school life, showing no interest in girls whatsoever, but despite a lack of romantic interest in the skinny boy, everyone was at least aware of him. While most of the boys in his class were going through their sexual awakening, Herb was experiencing two blossoming new passions of his own. His morbid fascinations seemed to publicly overshadow any sex drive that the teen was developing, and that was probably just as well for his safety. It was much less dangerous for a child to be the strange death-obsessed freak in the class than for him to be openly gay. Both would have evoked revulsion in the late 60s classroom, of course, but only one was an incitement to violence against him. It is unclear whether Herb even became aware of his attraction to men at this point in his life. He was experiencing so many conflicting emotions and impulses that it was likely drowned out until he reached a point of greater stability and clarity later in his life.

If he had been a less gregarious child then the sudden shift in his interests would probably have gone unnoticed, but young Herb had a great many friends that he chattered with incessantly. In an isolated, introverted child with a sense of shame or propriety, nobody would know the thought processes that were running through the pubescent mind. This was not the case with Herb. He would blurt out whatever was on his mind at any given moment, just the same way as he always had, but while previously all of his insights had been either comical or socially acceptable, now there was a steady stream of disturbing thoughts filtering through with the rest. One day, while playing with a group of boys, Herb paused and loudly wondered what urine would taste like. Whether it would taste better cold, or fresh from the source. The other boys were horrified, but they quickly wrote it off as Herb's sick sense of humour when he started chasing them around, begging for a drink.

In boys of that age, loud announcements about the most disgusting of subjects are considered to not only be normal but often hilarious, and the others soon made a game out of who could resist Herb's vile outbursts for the longest. Boys will be boys is an oft-repeated mantra that covers a whole multitude of sins. If a girl had exhibited even a fraction of Herb's abnormal behaviours, then she would have been delivered almost immediately to a psychiatric hospital. As Herb came to realise that his behaviour was not going to be chastised, he began to escalate. Rather than just thinking and talking about disgusting things, he began to do them.

Herb crouched down at the side of the road and stared at the dead crow. A cloud of flies lifted off it as he reached out towards it, and he shivered as the hollowed sockets of its eyes came into view. It was perfect. Reverently, he stroked the tiny feathers on its stomach. He gave a furtive glance up and down the road before leaning in closer to draw the stench of death deep into his lungs. He shuddered, and the tip of his tongue protruded from between his lips. Like he could taste death in the air. Like he wanted to drink it in. He pressed down harder on the crow, trying to force some last puff of breath from its broken body, but instead, he felt something moving beneath the surface. Maggots were under its skin, wriggling and dying as he crushed them against the bones of the corpse they called home. His hands were shaking, but he was not afraid. The rest of the world fell away until there were only him and the bird. He was finally at the height of his power. There was nobody here to tell him what to say, or how to think. There was nobody but him and the corpse in the entire universe, and he was the only one who was still alive. He was the one who made all the decisions. The corpse would lie how he wanted it, it would move only by the power of his hands. He was a god in this world he had created. He was the only god in the world that he had created. Nobody stood in judgement except for him, and he judged this rotten and bloated carcass to be delightful. He pressed harder and his fingers sunk into the decaying flesh. The black barrier of feathers began to part and the corruption gathered beneath the skin pooled around his fingertips. Wet and juicy. The dead were like ripe fruit. Forbidden fruit perhaps, but all the more delicious for it. Herb closed his eyes and just felt his fingers sinking into the corpse. Felt the dead flesh sucking at him as he pulled them back out. He was painfully hard and panting. There was a roaring sound in his ears as his blood thundered through. Just when he was on the cusp of that bright white moment of joy that he only ever found on the far side of death he heard a voice calling out.

'What the hell are you doing, Baumeister?'

His eyes snapped open and he plucked his fingers from the corpse with a disappointing squelch. He got his breath under control. He rearranged his face so that his arousal was less apparent. He turned to face the sound. 'Hey, Bill, how're you doing?'

Bill Donovan slowed his approach when he saw what Herb was hunkered down over. His brows drew down. 'What have you got there, Herb?'

Herb started to giggle and lifted a gore-smeared finger up to cross over his lips. 'Shh. Don't go spoiling the surprise now. This is for the grand finale.' He scooped up the bird, pausing to pick up its detached wing, and stuffed it into his jacket pocket while Bill tried to keep his disgust from showing. Letting Herb know that you were disgusted was a good way to become the target of his next practical joke. Bill didn't much fancy a neatly sliced worm sandwich for his lunch, he didn't fancy finding somebody had stuffed his gym kit down a toilet either. You couldn't be mad at Herb—he wasn't a bully like some of the kids at school, he was just funny. You couldn't be mad at a clown for spraying you with water and you couldn't be mad at Herb for pissing on your shoes. That was just the way he was.

On more than one occasion a dead crow was discovered on the teacher's desk, but despite everyone knowing that Herb was responsible, the students said nothing. He was the class clown. It was just a joke, it was just his sense of humour. Boys will be boys. Herb had become increasingly disruptive in class as time went on. His morbid fascinations crept into all his school work, and despite his obvious intelligence he was now beginning to fall behind his classmates due to his antics. The little secrets that his classmates kept for him as a matter of course weren't enough to protect him from discipline entirely. When a teacher arrived one morning to find that someone had urinated on her desk, there was no doubt in anyone's mind that Herb was responsible. When pressed, the other students in his class didn't roll over on their friend, but they did provide enough circumstantial evidence that the school were able to contact his parents with a fair assumption of his guilt.

His parents took the news about as well as anyone. In exchange for a promise from his father that professional advice would be sought about Herb's behaviour, the school allowed him to continue attending classes as normal. In a pattern that would continue for the rest of his life, his parents dodged the issue. Using Herbert Senior's medical connections, they created a circular paper trail of referrals to keep Herb out of the way of the system and hoped that the boy would just deal with his issues having been issued a stern warning.

This level of disregard may seem criminal by today's standards, but at this point in history, ignoring whatever problems Herb was experiencing may have been the kindest option. Psychiatry was still in its infancy at this point. There were very few accurate diagnoses, and even if they were somehow able to recognise Herb's true condition it would just result in his imprisonment for life. In all likelihood, if Herb had been put in front of the right kind of doctor they would not have been able to recognise his psychopathy and he would have been diagnosed with schizophrenia, as he was later in his life. It would be many years before psychopharmacology would create any sort of sustainable living situation for people suffering from schizophrenia. Herb would have been hospitalised and treated with electroconvulsive therapy to keep him sedate and pliant. The previous decade's fixation on lobotomisation couldn't have been much crueller a fate to inflict than what was done to the mentally ill during Herb's childhood.

His friends were now beginning to pull away from Herb, recognising that he was going beyond the realm of the acceptable even for a wealthy teenage boy. He became a taboo subject at the school, as the teachers tried to dance around his issues and his peers came to recognise that their friend might have a problem rather than a personality. His father had always been distant, but now he found even more excuses not to be in his son's company. The only one that seemed to truly care about Herb was his mother, and she was so appalled and disgusted by what now seemed to be a fundamental part of his personality that it reduced her to tears every time she looked at him. He learned to compartmentalise his life and to fake a semblance of rational behaviour. Psychopaths are often characterised as lacking any internal life: their only understanding of morality, empathy, and emotion are the outward expressions of those things, which they mimic to help them to blend in. At this stage, Herb still lacked the finesse to do so. He understood that his fixation on dead things was unacceptable, so he began to hide it. He understood that pursuing other men sexually was unacceptable, so he kept it secret. But he could see other people making jokes and being adored for it, and he could not make the distinction between the coarse and grotesque comments that he made and the more subdued humour of those around him. Exacerbating this problem was the fact that Herb's obscene comments were sometimes genuinely quite funny, even if the laughter sprang forth more often from outrage than from anything else. Because the rules of appropriate behaviour were constantly fluctuating, Herb could not determine when his jokes were going to be well received and when they were going to lead to ostracism. This was made even worse by the fact that Herb had always been the class clown, so when he was trying to win someone over his first tool was always his exuberant sense of humour. His limited successes only spurred him on to try harder with others, never fully understanding what the problem was. It was hardly surprising that socialisation became a source of frustration for him.

With less attention and less scrutiny, Herb was able to navigate his final school year in relative peace. Indulging in his dark obsessions privately, out of sight and out of mind. Still, he couldn't quite shrug off his innate desire to be a part of the group, to be popular and respected. Despite his more subdued attitude and repressing his more gruesome habits, he still made no inroads with the school football team or the tightly knit social order that had formed around it. He went through that final year alone, desperate for a fresh start.

Adrift

After school, Herb attended Indiana University. His family's reputation could do less to protect him, and things that people might accept of a teenager were considered contemptible. He was ostracised for his bizarre sense of humour, ignored in his classes, and treated like he was worth less than everyone else. He could not stand it. He gave up and returned home to live with his parents before the first semester was out.

His father was not impressed with this move. It isn't clear if he actually still held out hopes for Herb's future or if he was simply concerned about how his son's new slovenly attitude would reflect upon him in the local community. Initially, he badgered and harassed Herb to return to the university, but when even his imposing presence wasn't sufficient to cow Herb, he changed tact and made some calls about the community until he could find his son an entry-level job where he was unlikely to shame his family any further.

His first job was at the Indianapolis Star as a copy boy. He showed up to work each morning promptly and dressed in a suit that would have been more suitable for the editor. He was absolutely obsessed with success and the praise of his peers. He made many attempts to network with those in positions of power. He had very little success on the journalistic side of the business, but he soon laid down roots amongst the more business-oriented advertising department. His wheedling attempts to get praise from the rest of the paper's staff became irritating very quickly, but after the failure of college, he was determined to put in as much time and effort as was necessary to make himself popular this time around. He would still make his odd comments and offhand remarks, but thanks to the fairly twisted sense of humour that graced the advertising executive, Garry Donna, this sort of behaviour was tolerated, if not appreciated. Repeatedly through Herb's brief career at the paper, Donna would make excuses for his new protégé. 'That is just Herb,' he told the typing pool when Herb was heard laughing his way through a discussion of the decomposition of bodies with a journalist. 'That is just Herb,' he told everyone who came to his office complaining about the new guy's weird stares or uncomfortable jokes.

Donna may have appreciated Herb's sense of humour, but the boy was still far from accepted into the social hierarchy at the paper. Herb had recognised in school that he could not participate actively in sports, but now with some distance, he realised their power as a unifier and he cultivated an interest. When some of Donna's inner circle decided to attend a University of Indiana football game, Herb immediately offered them a ride in an attempt to ingratiate himself and slip into the fold. Any goodwill that he might have won himself was undone almost immediately by his over-the-top behaviour. He showed up to pick them up wearing a chauffeur's cap and joking about being at their service, which was already quite grating, but what really upset Donna's friends was the fact that Herb had pulled up to give them a lift in a hearse. Through his father's hospital connections, the boy had managed to purchase one from the local mortuary at a great discount. Donna was forced to turn to the dismayed group of sports fans and shrug as he had so many times before. 'That is just Herb.'

With what may have been his only chance to ingratiate himself into the Star's inner circle dashed by his own bizarre behaviour, Herb spiralled out of control. He was not getting the constant positive reinforcement that he craved. He was barely receiving the respect that he felt was due to him as a copy boy. He became increasingly surly and introverted. The people who he once lavished with praise and flattery he instead snubbed. It was clear to him that he was never going to be a success at the Indianapolis Star. So confronted with a situation that he was not emotionally equipped to deal with, Herb did what he always did. He quit.

If his father had been furious about Herb dropping out of college, that was nothing compared to his response to the very public shame that followed the family after Herb's first attempt at a career. With his ego in tatters after the fiasco at the newspaper, Herb was more pliable to his father's demands this time around. He was sent back to the university, not to complete an entire semester but to complete just a single class, to prove that he was capable and worthy of further help. Given the selection of any course on the university's prospectus, Herb quickly narrowed in on a course about human anatomy. His father took this as a good sign that his son might finally be following in his footsteps and pursuing a worthwhile career in medicine. In fact, it was just Herb's morbid fixation with dead bodies raising its head once again. He had sincerely hoped to perform an autopsy as a part of his course and was quietly dismayed when it became clear that the closest he would be coming to a dead body was the pictures in his textbook.

Despite the course lacking in the practical skills that Herb was hoping to cultivate, he still dutifully attended, and once he had switched his focus from socialisation to his studies he actually excelled. With his head down and less of his energy being expended on attracting attention, Herb's more flamboyant personality traits snuck under the radar. If anyone remembered the grating and morbid Herb Baumeister from the start of the year, they were not able to match that memory to the calm and collected young man who now attended the school, always beautifully presented in a clean pressed suit. His father was somewhat satisfied with his son's new sombre demeanour and pleased to see some of the competitive spirit returning to him after so long without any victories in his life.

With this newfound confidence, Herb began visiting Indianapolis in the evenings, visiting gay bars and drag acts. He travelled incognito, using public transportation rather than his rather noticeable hearse, and thanks to the kindness of the local gay scene he went almost entirely unobserved throughout his fleeting visits. There was no shortage of questioning young men in Indianapolis who just wanted a glimpse of what their lives could be like. He was reluctant to bond with the people here, aware dimly that they were as forbidden as the corpses that he liked to toy with, albeit in a different way. He dipped his toes into the water and found a vibrant community of people who he could have found kinship with if he was willing to give up on his obsession with popularity and ambition. Soon his visits became more frequent and other regulars started to acknowledge him. He made some casual friends amongst them. People who cackled along with his sordid jokes and disturbing observations. His life was already compartmentalised between his private excursions away from civilisation and his public life—it took barely any effort at all to fragment it further.

His social life began to garner some interest from his father. He was only attending a single class at college and the rest of his time seemed to be wasted on frivolity. With scrutiny of his two secret lives being threatened, Herb picked up an extracurricular activity that he knew would please his father and suit his own interests, too. He joined the university's Young Republicans Club. Despite the obvious contradictions of his carefully segregated lifestyles and interests, his extreme right-wing politics made him a great fit for the group. Because nobody in the organisation joked around at any time, Herb was able to navigate the social aspect of the group without causing offence, and for the first time since his arrival at the university, his family's wealth and position in town were once again being considered. In a way, it was a return to the simplicity of his youth. Right and wrong were black and white, people weren't offended by everything that he said and he was treated with some measure of respect.

Without his odious personality to ward people off, Herb started to garner the attention of some of the young ladies at the club. In particular, he caught the eye of Juliana Saiter, a high school English teacher who was attending classes at the university part-time. With his buttoned-down style of dress and his mid-western looks, he was considered to be pretty handsome within that circle. Between that, their shared interest in cars, and Julie's shared political views, it seemed like a good match—something that even Herb seemed to be aware of.

He stood at a crossroads in his life. In one direction was the straight and narrow path that his father prescribed for him. Marriage to Julie and his very own pursuit of the American Dream. On the other side were his hidden alternate personas, the corpse-defiling morbid obsessive and the flamboyant gay party boy. For someone with a simplistic view of the world, the decision was simple. He took the 'good' path that would lead him away from temptation. He would crush down any hint of his real self and pursue his goals. He began dating Julie, cut off all ties to the gay scene, stopped going for his 'walks' away from prying eyes, and to an outside observer, he became a decent law-abiding citizen.

With newfound confidence in his ability to navigate the 'normal' world, Herb had enough confidence to push back against his father in a more meaningful way. He had no interest in academia and he did not believe that any qualification was going to help him with the goals that he was trying to pursue in life. Herb wanted to surpass the level of wealth that his father had accrued for himself over the course of his lifetime. The acquisition of wealth seemed to be a particularly popular goal amongst conservatives growing up amidst the hazy hippy counter-culture of the 70s. They felt like the majority of their generation had abandoned their posts and that it left the world rife with opportunity for the few people who were willing to put the necessary work in. The fact that he was attempting to challenge his father, a man who exerted considerable influence over him, is pretty simple to understand. Realising that the man he was dealing with was no longer the broken boy who had come limping home from college the first time, Herb's father began reaching out to his contacts around Indianapolis in search of a job where Herb might apply his newfound confidence in the pursuit of his laudable goals.

The Baumeister's met Julie early in the courtship. Herb was overeager to show off his girlfriend and prove his masculinity to his father. The older man was delighted, taking Julie as another sign that Herb was finally getting his life in order. Herb's mother was less pleased. She was torn between her maternal instincts towards Herb—which made her think that this school teacher wasn't nearly good enough for her perfect son—and her learned revulsion towards Herb that made her want to warn the poor girl off. In the end, Elizabeth Baumeister kept her mouth shut, assuming that the relationship would soon run its course and confident that if it became necessary to pay the girl hush money after she witnessed some of Herb's unsavoury interests, that Julie could be cheaply bought.

There were a string of false starts and failed interviews for Herb as he tried to start down the road towards prosperity. His father's influence in Indianapolis was far-reaching, but for all of his wealth and connections, he had to contend with the unfortunate reality of Herb himself. Herb was handsome by the standards of the day. He presented himself well, and his academic failure could very easily be interpreted as a young man trying to find the right path for himself. Even his intensity could be mistaken for a sort of magnetic charisma if viewed only in a snapshot. Yet still, something about him seemed to rub interviewers the wrong way. While his appearance, his family, and their position in the community signalled stability, Herb himself did not. Between his lack of empathy and his 'sense of humour,' Herb exuded an aura of chaos. If given enough time to prove himself in the workplace focusing on an actual job, the irregularities could have been smoothed over, but in the brief snapshot of a job interview, the clash between what Herb presented himself as and what they expected was too much for the interviewers to overcome.

Herb's relationship with Julie was rapidly becoming the only point of stability in his life. Both of his parents were sources of stress and anguish respectively. His siblings had all distanced themselves from him following his social ostracism back in school and Herb had neither the skills nor the inclination to mend those relationships. They continued to date as he worked his way through trial periods in several small businesses and eventually, with nothing else to hold onto and a romantic ideal rooted deeply in his heart, Herb asked her to marry him.

Original Prankster

Despite his parents' initial reluctance at such a short courtship period, the wedding was planned and went ahead in November of 1971, at the United Methodist Church in Indianapolis. The mutual friend who had introduced Herb and Julie was in attendance, along with all their other Young Republican friends, the social network that would one day grow to sustain the Baumeister's in the same way that Herb Senior's connections had helped him to advance in life. On top of that already expansive circle of people, all of Herb and Julie's extended family were in attendance, along with any important friends of Herb's parents. For the wealthy of Indianapolis, social events like the weddings of their children were vital to bolstering their ties to one another, to foster a sense of community and family rather than the competition that was so often their first impulse. The pressure to be perfect was immense. At a glance, Herb did not seem to be feeling any pressure at all. Julie looked as nervous as any bride has ever been, but Herb was calm, collected, and charming in a way that would have surprised anyone who knew him from school. When put into an unfamiliar social situation, or placed in a position where he was lacking in confidence, Herb would now default to a serious and calm demeanour. It was only when he felt sure of himself that his comedic outbursts would be unleashed.

Many of the Baumeister's' family and friends only remembered Herb from his youthful indiscretions; their mental image of him was as a bizarre delinquent. This very public showing of his new mature attitude won many of them over, and the interview offers began flowing in regularly after the wedding. With a small gift from his parents, the promise of forthcoming work, and Julie's teaching wages, the two were able to take out a mortgage on a small house in the suburbs, where they settled after the big event itself. Which was when Herb finally ran out of excuses.

Up until now, their strict Christian upbringing had protected Herb from Julie's carnal advances, but now that they were married he was entirely out of excuses if he wanted to keep his charade of heterosexuality going. In the world outside of their bedroom, they were the perfect couple. They spent all of their time together, even working in the garden together to show themselves off to the neighbourhood. She would trim the edges while he cut the grass. She would plant the flowers as he picked the weeds. All of their free time was shared, an incredible crutch for Herb in his struggles to stick to his daytime life rather than falling back into old habits. That level of co-dependency might be considered unhealthy by today's standards, but for both of the Baumeisters, it was ideal. To people who grew up fixated on the image of the 1950s atomic family ideal, it was a dream come true. Inside the home Herb continued with the same charade, lavishing attention and affection on his new wife, but within the bedroom, he became cold, withdrawn and distant. He would get changed in the bathroom, ensuring that he was never naked in the same room as Julie, and doing his best to contain his revulsion when she approached him without clothing on. In the early days, she thought he was being respectful, then that he was shy or bashful. As she became more aggressive in her attempts to bed her husband, he withdrew further until the previous warmth that she had experienced in their married life became a memory.

With no release from the constant observation of Julie, and the pressure to function sexually with a woman that he had no attraction to, Herb began to crack. He became increasingly normal and quiet as the tension mounted. The more that his mental health suffered, the less that any instability became visible. It was only when his father came to visit the newlyweds six months into their cohabitation that anyone realised that there was a problem at all. The men did not argue throughout Herb Senior's entire visit, and when prompted to follow up on some of the interviews his father had secured for him, he passively agreed to whatever was asked of him. In less than 24 hours, his father had him committed to a mental institution with Julie's blessing.

While Herb voluntarily entered the facility for treatment of his depression, it did not take long into his two-month visit before the doctors began to realise that they were dealing with an entirely different set of issues. Initially, the strange compartmentalisation of his dark impulses—impulses he wouldn't even discuss with the doctors treating him—led them to believe that he was a schizophrenic who used this mental barrier as a means to protect himself from his hallucinations and harmful ideation. Schizophrenia tended to be the catchall diagnosis for the vast majority of unusual conditions at the time, but thanks to the sensationalism of several high-profile cases of 'multiple personality disorder,' this diagnosis was later amended. It should be noted that at the time, there were no diagnosis criteria for multiple personalities, and as time and science have progressed it has been decided that the diagnosis of 'multiple personalities' has consistently been incorrect, with only two or three cases throughout history being considered genuine, and many better explanations for those symptoms being offered with different diagnoses.

For Herb, the diagnosis was the biggest relief of his life because it completely absolved him of all responsibility. It wasn't him who wanted to have sex with men, it was someone else who just so happened to inhabit his body. It wasn't him who wanted to play with dead bodies, it was someone else. Herb was harmless, wouldn't hurt a fly. The desire to have everyone who had ever crossed him laid out as corpses in his own charnel house didn't belong to Herb. It was somebody else who wanted to feel the cold bodies beneath his hands, powerless and pliable. Herb was a good person. He wouldn't want any of those things.

Just receiving the diagnosis was enough to break Herb out of the spiral of depression and stress that had been consuming him ever since he started suppressing his darker impulses. If he was not responsible for his actions, then he no longer had to worry about them. Seeing his son returned to vibrant life and fearing that a longer stay would allow the local community to catch wind of Herb's institutionalisation, his father had him discharged. While there were drug therapies for schizophrenia becoming available by this point, many in the medical community—Herb Senior included—felt that they were just a crutch for the weak-willed. If you think the stigma against mental health now is bad, consider that most of the doctors in the 70s had been taught that most mental illness was a product of moral failing.

Herb returned to the waiting arms of his beloved wife. She was absolutely delighted to have him home and back to his old self. With his newly integrated psyche, he was able to perform sexually for the first time. Before, he had been cutting himself off from the fantasies that allowed him to get excited, but now that there was no more guilt he was able to function to at least some degree. He still wouldn't let Julie see him naked, and all their activities had to be carried out in total darkness. She came to believe that this odd reluctance was a holdover from his school days. She knew that he had not been athletic as a child, although the full breadth of his pariah-dom was kept secret from her to avoid having to explain too much. In exchange for finally living the life that she believed was both her right and her duty, Julie would have accepted far stranger things. Indeed, whenever the two of them disagreed on any part of their life, she seemed to take pleasure in deferring to Herb, her newly assertive husband who seemed to be in control of everything, at least in the beginning of their marriage. As a part of his new, healthy self, Herb announced that he was going to start spending some time alone with his thoughts. He was going to take long drives, go for walks in nature, spend time in the library, or try to reconnect with old friends. In her blissful haze, Julie accepted all of this without question.

With renewed vigour, Herb returned to working life. His father had secured him a job at the Bureau of Motor Vehicles before his brief stint in the institution, and the entry-level position was still sitting open for him. The calm and collected version of Herb presented himself for work on the first day, but within a few weeks, he was learning the ropes and confident enough to ease off his disguise. He had become savvier over the years, and he did not launch so readily into his old jokes and morbid mumblings. The first time that most of his co-workers even realised he was there was when he started loudly berating them for simple mistakes. Most of them were so taken aback by the sudden volume that they didn't even attempt to mount a defence and the few that did found that there was little that could be done to calm the young man once he had started his rambling. Worse still, they couldn't even return the favour because he was extremely careful to complete all of his work perfectly. Any attempt to complain to their superiors was met with condescension. After all, they had made the very mistakes that he was accusing them of, and if he was passionate about the work then that was surely a positive thing. He was soon loathed by his contemporaries, but his superiors took his play-acting of 'supervisor behaviour' and outbursts, along with his impeccable work ethic, to be signs that he was management material. He was quietly moved onto the fast track for promotion and probably would have moved up the ranks much sooner if his sense of propriety had been slightly better attuned.

Herb had not returned to the wilderness, as he had promised his wife. Instead, he was spending more and more of his time on the gay scene. Because of the way that he had compartmentalised his life, he genuinely believed that repressing his sexuality was exactly the same as repressing his far darker impulses. He believed that spending time in gay bars hitting on men was going to provide him with the release that he needed, but early on he discovered that this was not the case. He had some sexual encounters with other men, but they did not give him the satisfaction that he was expecting. Sex did not give him the satisfaction that society had told him it would. Every encounter just seemed to underline the fact that there was something wrong with him. Both the conservative culture that he had grown up in and the gay subculture of Indianapolis attached massive significance to sex, and the fact that this supposedly life-changing activity wasn't changing Herb's life was a source of massive frustration for him.

Herb didn't even know this guy's name, but he was young, willing, and pathetic enough that the tiny bit of cash that Herb had been flashing in the bar had caught his attention. He kept flipping his blond mop of hair back out of his eyes and fluttering his eyelashes like he had learned to flirt from an old black and white movie. Whatever shyness he might have been trying to fake for Herb vanished once they got to the motel. Herb handed over the cash and the boy walked right up to the receptionist to book a room while Herb stayed outside heaving in the warm summer night air and trying to keep the images of pale bodies from flickering through his mind. He blamed it on the strobing lights in the nightclubs, the flashes of bare skin that they showed, frozen in the moment. He could feel the bones of dead birds between his fingers when he saw them, felt the weakness of them flexing beneath the pressure of his hands. So fragile. So easily broken. The blond came out of reception with a key dangling from his finger and Herb's change squirrelled away in his pocket. It was pocket change and Herb had bigger fish to fry tonight. Herb kept his hands in front of him, holding one with the other to keep himself from reaching out and giving any sign of impropriety. He was a slow learner, but after this long, he was starting to develop a little bit of restraint and caution. All it would take was the wrong set of eyes to be looking in the wrong direction at the wrong moment and his carefully constructed house of lies would come tumbling down.

Inside the motel room, all the restraint fell away and he finally had the boy in his hands. Herb squeezed his arms and felt the muscles shift beneath the surface. Then it all started to go wrong. The boy was kissing him. His mouth was open and the boy's tongue was pushing inside. Herb froze as that slug-like mass of muscle slithered across the backs of his teeth. He shuddered and it was taken as further invitation. The kiss felt like being mauled. Like something without teeth was trying to bite his face off his body. In an instant, the boy went from being the most delectable treat Herb had ever laid eyes on to being loathsome. When he surged forward and pinned Herb to the door, grinding up against him, it was almost too much to bear. A sob surged up in Herb's throat and he pushed back, sending the kid stumbling back to land on the bed. His lips looked swollen like Herb had hit him. For a moment, Herb wanted to hit him— he even felt his fist tightening of its own accord. He was ruining it.

This idiot was ruining everything, with his mussed-up hair and his punch-drunk lips lolling open and the tantalising glimpse of darkness just inside. Herb closed the distance in two steps and almost lifted the boy off the bed as he wrestled with his belt. 'You wanna fuck me?' Herb didn't answer, he just tore the trousers down the kid's tanned legs and groaned at the sight of him bared beneath him. 'Do it. Fuck me. Come on. Do it.'

Herb had a condom in his pocket and it was the work of two practised moments to get it on, but the next part couldn't be rushed. Herb forced the boy's legs up off the bed and flinched as his face got too close for comfort. He slicked his fingers with the little jar of Vaseline in his pocket and he tried his best to ignore the constant litany from the boy as he pushed his fingers inside him. 'Oh yes. Oh. Fuck me. Yes.'

It was wrong. His fingers were sinking into flesh like he always fantasised about, but the meat was too hot. It was all too hot. Herb was sweating and gasping. He felt like his fingers were burning inside this stupid pretty boy when everything should have been perfect and calm. The world was not falling away. The darkness pressing in around him was ruined by the flicker of neon through the poorly shrouded windows of the motel room. The mattress springs were pinging and creaking beneath them. His fingers felt like they were seared and he couldn't stand another moment of touching the heat inside the boy, so he abandoned any other preparation and dove right in. It got worse from there. The boy wouldn't stay still. Even pinned with his knees on his chest he writhed and moaned and begged and cajoled and it was like fucking Julie all over again. A worthless animal rutting against him. This was meant to be his time. He was meant to be alone in the dark place with all of the power to do whatever he wanted and instead... 'Yes. Fuck me harder. Do it. Do it baby.'

Bile roiled in Herb's stomach. The beers he had forced down in the bar were churning too. He was going to throw up on this worthless animal if he didn't close his eyes.

Even with them shut there were the noises and the heat. It was only when he heard the softer sounds underneath the braying voice of the boy that he felt the chaos easing away from the edges of his senses. The soft slapping of skin on skin. The liquid sounds of a body moving inside another one. The displacement of fluids in the corpse. The shifting of gases and the—insufferable talking. 'Yes. Yes. Yes.'

It isn't like they have anything to say to each other. It isn't like the boy is saying anything at all. He is just ruining everything because he can't shut his damned mouth and enjoy the experience. He had been trained to talk, to make himself the centre of attention. To make sure that Herb knew that he was meeting his needs. Herb didn't care about meeting his needs. He didn't care about pleasing anyone except himself and the constant braying was maddening. Herb let go of the boy's legs, letting them flop down against his shoulders and setting off a whole new set of stupid, endlessly repeated catchphrases. Herb's free hands slipped up between the boy's legs, wrinkled their way up his t-shirt and pressed down firmly on his collarbones. He could feel the boy breathing hard, swollen lungs pressing his bones up against Herb's hands. He hated it.

His hands slipped up a little higher and closed around the boy's throat and suddenly the room was quiet. Herb blinked his eyes open, startled by the sudden silence and frightened at what his fury might have driven his hands to do while he was trying to drift away. But the boy was still breathing, still writhing and shifting when Herb just wanted him to stay where he had been put. There were still sounds coming out of his mouth but they were body sounds, not forced and false. The woof of air driven out of his lungs every time Herb slammed into him. The soft moans of satisfaction were almost tolerable. They sounded like a death rattle. Like the times that Herb had found bodies so fresh that he could still squeeze that last drop of life out of them. Herb shuddered, and this time it wasn't repressed suffering. He flexed his fingers and drew a high desperate moan out of the boy. All of the pressure, all of the fight, left him. He became everything that Herb wanted him to be for just a moment. He was still and pliant. Perfect and beautiful. Then he started talking again and spoiled the moment. 'Choke me harder. Please baby. Do it harder.' Herb grit his teeth and hammered into the other man, suddenly desperate to get this over with and get out as fast as he could.

Sex with Julie was an unpleasant chore that he forced himself through for the purpose of maintaining their charade of a life together. Sex with the men from the clubs was unfulfilling because instead of being interested in his pleasure they were fixated on their own. The sense of entitlement that had plagued Herb throughout his life was just as present in his back-alley liaisons as it was in his office squabbles. Like a true psychopath, he wanted the world to revolve around him. He wanted other people to be his playthings, not his equals.

Compartmentalisation remained a problem for Herb. Some things were distinct and clear to him. He could not bring his gay life into his conservative house. He could not bring his morbid fascinations into the office. But other things were shakier: could he talk about the office at home? Would some of his sick jokes amuse Julie? Could some fringe benefits of his gay lifestyle be useful in breaking through the social barriers that he encountered at the office? While Julie was tolerant of his humour and seemed to enjoy trading work stories with her husband, his attempts to bring his exuberant and bubbly gay personality into the office were ill-judged. His flamboyant jokes fell on deaf ears. His practical jokes were considered utterly tasteless at best and as bullying at worst. One Christmas he gave out cards with a picture of himself posing with a festive drag queen, leading to a great deal of muttering around the water cooler that he might be a closeted homosexual himself. This set back his pursuit of promotion considerably, and it was only after almost a decade of working in the Bureau that he finally received the promotion that he believed was his right.

While for most men this would have been a time of jubilation and satisfaction, Herb immediately came into conflict with his new boss. While he had perfected his supervisor act for his subordinates, he had no idea how to socialise with someone who was meant to be his superior, which led to considerable butting of heads as he tried to treat his boss like everyone else and was admonished for his rudeness. Once again, the actual work was Herb's saving grace. Despite his unpleasant personality, he was one of the best workers in the whole BMV, and his constant, hawk-like attention to detail and his vitriol at any error—no matter how tiny—led to the people working under him producing some of the best results, too. No matter how much he grated on his boss's nerves, the bottom line was that he was the best person for the job and they had no grounds to get rid of him.

Julie had given up work during Herb's slow climb through the ranks, and they had moved into a bigger house, suitable for raising a family. Getting pregnant was not easy for the couple, mainly because Herb obstinately refused to have sex with his wife and the more pressure that she put on him, the more he resisted her. In pursuit of his own sexual satisfaction, Herb had begun to frequent male prostitutes in the city, trying to find what he was looking for in a partner. There were a few reports filed with the police about a man getting rough with the prostitutes, but it blended into the background noise of regular criminal investigation, never even making it to the press. Herb had withdrawn almost entirely from the gay scene of the city and he was forgotten about by his old friends quite rapidly, with the assumption that he had either moved away or slipped so far back into the closet that even his clandestine trips to the clubs were too much for him to cope with. It was sad but hardly unheard of.

Despite the difficulties involved, Julie was able to conceive several times over the decade of Herb's employment at the BMV. The pair had three children: Marie, the eldest, was born in 1979, almost a decade after the couple married. Two years later his only son, Erich, followed. Finally, their youngest, Emily, was born three years later. Fatherhood cut into Herb's free time in an entirely unexpected way. While he may have tried to emulate his father's distant behaviour, he lacked the necessary temperament to completely withdraw from his children. By all accounts, he was a doting father, pouring all the affection that he withheld from his wife into the kids. He was always generous to his children, both with the limited budget available in the early years of their lives and more importantly, with his time. Despite being painfully aware of his own need for time away from the family to indulge his darker impulses, he persisted in spending most of his time at home with the kids when he was not working. It was as if he was trying to prevent them from ending up like him, driven by hatred for their own father.

Between the stress of work and his struggles at home, Herb found that he needed some sort of outlet for all of this frustration. As he had when confronted with an unassailable authority figure in his childhood, Herb sought out a way to release some of that tension—a way to humiliate and degrade his boss that wouldn't require much thought, forward planning, or navigating the social minefields of office politics. He started urinating on his boss' desk. When he was in school and behaving like this, he was immediately punished. The other children recognised that his behaviour had become too transgressive and they turned on him. In the workplace, however, where Herb was already loathed by everyone, there was nothing but silent simmering outrage. While suspicion was certainly enough to get a child in trouble, without incontrovertible proof, nobody wanted to go up against Herb or the lawsuits he would likely levy against the Bureau if they tried to dismiss him unfairly. After months of coming in to urine soaked stationery, Herb's boss seemed to quietly accept the situation. Just another little quirk of Herb's that had to be tolerated to get the work done. With silence from management, there came speculation that perhaps it was someone else, that Herb was too obvious a suspect. A piss-soaked desk became the centre of office gossip for months. In all likelihood, the situation could have gone on forever, except that one day a letter to the governor of Indiana was left on his boss' desk and was doused in urine along with everything else. Apparently, this was a step too far, while the previous urination was not. Herb was quietly dismissed the same day with a simple offer: if he left now without making a fuss, then his toilet habits would not become public knowledge. This brought an end to Herb's 'practical jokes' for the foreseeable future.

The Good Years

Herb's father arrived shortly after he parted ways with the BMV. The pickings were much slimmer when it came to jobs this time around. Those who hadn't already been burned by Herb's antics were extremely reluctant to take him on given the rumours that were circulating about him. It had been too long since the wedding. Too long since the Baumeisters had put on a display of normalcy for the community, and now the truth was starting to slip through. With the children a little older, Julie returned to teaching part-time to supplement their income. Herb took on some odd jobs over the course of a year, generally sales roles that involved a lot of travelling. This time away from the family seemed to do wonders for maintaining his mental equilibrium, so despite his making barely enough to cover their bills, Julie encouraged him to pursue success down that road. Eventually, he returned to Indianapolis on a full-time basis, claiming to miss his wife and children too much. His father scraped the bottom of the barrel to find him a job and eventually landed him an entry-level position as a sales clerk in a thrift store. If Herb had ever taken the time to lay out a plan for his life, some sort of roadmap for the meteoric rise to success that he expected to experience, then it is probably safe to say that working in a thrift shop did not feature in those plans.

From the very beginning, he felt like his immense talents were being wasted in a menial and degrading job. The longer that he spent working in the thrift shop, the more glaring the management's flaws became to him. The thrift store business had the potential to be incredibly profitable with only a little bit of effort, but his new boss seemed unwilling to put in that effort and actively discouraged Herb from taking initiative himself. Two years into his tenure, at about the time that he usually would have started urinating all over the shop, Herb was forced to take some time off work after receiving some shocking news. His father had just passed away.

In the lives of many killers, there is a turning point, a stressor that unlocks their murderous instincts and looking back at the life of Herb Baumeister up until this point you might suspect that it arrived with the death of his father. Herbert Senior was the focus of so much of his son's anger. His unattainable goal of overwhelming fiscal success was driven entirely by attempts to best the old man. Every accomplishment was just another attempt at gaining his distant father's approval. With his death, Herbert Senior put an end to all of that. He would never see his son best him. He would never give the unconditional love and admiration that Herb was seeking. Emotionally, this was now a dead end. On the other hand, any restraint that Herb might have shown in his life to prevent his father from discovering his secret shame was now thoroughly undone. It was as if God was no longer watching.

Herb did not instantly spiral out of control. In fact, after the funeral arrangements were made and Julie tried to comfort him, he was instead elated with newly realised ambition. Both of them had always dreamed of owning their own business and pursuing the American Dream, but now Herb had an idea for how that might be achieved. His time working in the thrift shop had shown him the boundless potential of that sort of business. A thrift shop under intelligent management is a license to print money. Stock is bought in for a fraction of its worth and sold on at massive profit margins, and all that it takes is an eye for items of value to transform a middling business into a wildly successful one. The fact that most thrift shops come with backing from a charity to give them credibility along with some promotional and financial assistance was just a bonus for the duo. In the months that followed, they would take trips all over Indiana and Ohio to visit auctions and consider the saleable quality of potential job lots. By the time that Herb had reached the end of his third year working in the thrift shop, he was certain that he had learned all that he was ever going to, so he approached his widowed mother to ask for a small loan to get the business started. Had his father been alive, he would have likely been stonewalled and left with nothing, but his mother still carried lingering guilt from the way that she had rejected her son when he was going through his 'difficult phase' in his teenage years. She signed a cheque for the not insubstantial sum of $4000 dollars to help them secure a location and used her contacts to put the couple in touch with some of the local charities that might be interested in supporting them. Herb gave his notice the very next day and the couple set out on their new venture together.

The "Sav-A-Lot" thrift store opened its doors in 1988 at a prime location on 46th street. They had the backing of the Children's Bureau of Indianapolis, a centenarian charity that benefitted local families, and when customers first arrived they were shocked at how organised and clean the place was compared to the other local thrift stores. Selling household goods, clothing, and other second-hand items, the store swiftly became a favourite shopping location for the poorer elements of the city. The Bureau, who had difficulty raising funds in the past, was delighted with the way that Herb and Julie were managing things. In exchange for the tax benefits of being affiliated with the charity and the social benefits of coming under their umbrella, the Baumeisters paid along a percentage of their sales to the charity, resulting in some very happy administrators, indeed, after the shop turned a profit of $50,000 in its first year. It was not long into the second year of business that the Baumeisters opened up a second location and the couple were forced to split up to manage one each, at least until the third year when they hired competent enough staff to take over the day-to-day running of things.

With these successes under their belt, in 1991 the Baumeisters moved out of the city into the fashionable Westfield District in Hamilton County, almost 20 miles from Indianapolis proper. They mortgaged an elegant and expansive Tudor-style mansion called Fox Hollow Farms. The property had four bedrooms, an indoor swimming pool, a riding stable, and over eighteen acres of land for the children to play on. It was the kind of tranquil country living that Julie had always dreamed of and thanks to Herb, those dreams were finally coming true. They may have only had sex six times in their entire marriage, but what did that matter compared to real, tangible things like the business of her dreams, the house of her dreams, and the lifestyle that she had always longed for.

Luxury had arrived and it was here to stay. Between their life at Fox Hollow Farm and the long summers that she spent with the children and Herb's mother lounging around her retirement condo by Lake Wawasee, it was all too easy for Julie to crush down any suspicions that she might have harboured about her husband. Whether they were about the long but strangely fruitless business trips that he took out to Ohio, the way that he had to stay in town during their visits to his mother to take care of their business interests, or the long drives that he still took in the evenings to gather his thoughts. None of that mattered. She had what she wanted.

The I-70 Strangler

Herb did not suddenly lose his mind and start killing people when his father died—because he had already found an outlet for his darkest impulses. During his time working as a travelling salesman he was constantly running up and down the I-70 visiting potential clients across three states. He was living on a very limited budget during those long months on the road, staying in the cheapest and sleaziest hotels and living off diner food. It was like a completely different world from the one back home: the people were different, the places were different. While Herb had to slap on a mask of decency and normalcy when he was visiting his clients, out on the road and in the dark and dingy places that he stopped, he could finally be his true self. Unseen by anyone that mattered. He could make his vile jokes to the truckers and waitresses without anyone raising an eyebrow. In the long periods of solitude when he was behind the wheel he could slip away into his fantasies where death and sex blended together seamlessly. It was a place where his daytime life as an upstanding member of the community seemed more like a bad dream than a reality that he had to endure.

Still, Herb was never the solitary type. He needed to be the centre of attention. It was only a few weeks into his travels that he started picking up hitchhikers. The first few times he did it, he genuinely just wanted company. The hitchhiker had to endure his constant rambling tirades, his 'jokes' and his abrasive personality in exchange for their ride, but as frightening as that might have become, he never laid a hand on them. As with every other sphere that Herb navigated, it took him some time to acclimate to this new one where he could be his authentic self. It took time for him to gain enough confidence to demand sex from one of the hitchhiking boys in exchange for taking them where they wanted to go. The first few attempts were abortive. He spluttered out his demands before the boys were in the car and his fear of discovery prompted him to speed off before he had even gotten an answer. Herb was nothing if not persistent.

Out here in the liminal space between cities, Herb finally felt like himself. The world narrowed down to the size of the cabin of his car and only darkness and the rolling road existed outside of that. He didn't have to fear every tiny mistake out here. He could be who he wanted when he wanted, and he could make as many mistakes as he needed to without them ever coming back to haunt him. Out here in the wide anonymous expanse of middle America, he was nobody and everybody. He had been through his practice runs, he had built up his confidence with front seat fumbles and back seat grunting. He had learned to let just a little part of his savage nature slip out from behind the mask of sanity once he had one of those sweet hitchhiking boys in his front seat. 'You know that nobody rides for free. You pay for gas or you pay in ass.'

He couldn't believe his own daring. He couldn't believe the degrading words that slipped out of his mouth so easily. Herb was glad that it wasn't him saying those awful filthy things. He was so relieved that there was someone else who could slip out from behind the solid wall in his mind and slide into his skin and show that little sharp smile to the boys and let them know that there was no way in hell they were getting out of his car without getting fucked first. These lost boys were quick to give it up and the ones that weren't caught a glimpse of the pistol in his glove box and lost their nerve and their inhibitions quicker than they could slip their pants down.

Herb had been building his confidence through these long lonely months in the middle of nowhere. Each time that he picked up a boy it got a little bit easier to force their head down into his lap as he drove along. Some of the boys out here knew his face now and he didn't give a damn. They weren't real people any more than this long stretch of empty interstate was a real place: they were just shadow puppets, ideas of people that ought to exist being piped in from somewhere to fill up the space. Herb liked it when they knew him, when they recognised him for what he truly was but still came climbing into his car as willingly as a virgin to her wedding bed. They knew what he was going to do to them. They knew he was going to have them at his mercy, and even so, they still submitted to him. Some of them had to like it. Some of them had nothing good in their life worth hanging on to. He was a real man, a man who was going to make something out of his life and they were nothing but warm bodies that he could use to scratch an itch.

Even when he was back at home Herb was dreaming about these lost boys now. The fantasies were mingling with the dreams from his adolescence. He imagined the hitchers were road kill. Corpses scattered by the roadside for the curious little boys to play with. Sometimes they were crow-faced and black with feathers. Sometimes they were perfect and pale, as cold as the moonlight streaming down from the empty sky above. When he woke up from those dreams, he would sometimes go as far as crossing the room to Julie's bed. He never got as far as waking her up. He knew that when he felt this desperate need for release his wife was meant to be his outlet, but just looking at the lumpy shape of her under the blankets was enough to dampen his lust. He spent those long nights at home lying awake, staring up at the ceiling and plotting out his next adventure out in the wilds. For all that he looked like a timid suburban Republican, Herb knew more about sex than anyone in his social circles had a right to. He knew the depths of depravity that men would go to for a rush. The kinky sex that straight people were only just starting to discover in the subcultures of the 70s had originated in the gay scene, and while married couples were just starting to realise that spankings might be more than just discipline for kids, the gay community had already graduated to erotic asphyxiation.

Herb had done it himself once or twice during his hook-ups, more by accident than intentionally, trying to silence the ceaseless noise that burst out of his casual partner as he tried to have his way with him. He knew just how easy it would be to go on squeezing. To go from having his beautiful lost boys still writhing and resisting as he raped them in that back seat to having the lifeless dolls that he had always dreamed of. All it would take would be a little more pressure, a little more time, then he could have anything that he wanted. He wouldn't have to ask permission, he wouldn't have to say please and thank you. He could make them into the perfect lovers. Still and cold. Nothing but flesh for his pleasure.

There was nothing special about this trip. The stars weren't aligned in some special way and nothing particularly interesting was happening in Herb's life. It was just another run to some nowhere town to sell some boring products that Herb could barely remember the name of most days. He found the hiker at a petrol station on the interstate, some long-haired, dark-eyed boy who couldn't have been out of his teens. He was familiar enough that Herb didn't even give it a second thought before ushering him into the car and pulling away. There wasn't any need for words beyond those first few exchanges of pure information. The destination they were headed for. The destination that the boy wanted to reach. Both lined up closely enough that they didn't have to go through pointless negotiation before Herb reached out and dragged the boy by the back of his head to an inch above his fly. They stayed there, frozen for a moment before Herb growled, 'It isn't going to suck itself.'

That seemed to be enough to shake the hitcher out of whatever safe place he had retreated to in his head. His hands moved with confidence, unzipping Herb's fly and deftly pulling him out. They made it a good few miles before Herb started to feel the first pangs of excitement. It had all become routine by now. The boys with the sad eyes and the warm lips. He made it another few miles before he sighed and pulled over onto a dusty patch by the side of the road. When they stopped the hitcher tried to go to town on him, but Herb tangled his fingers up in the boy's greasy hair and dragged him off, gasping for air. 'Into the back. I've got bigger plans for you.'

He moved slowly when he opened the glove box to fetch out the condom and Vaseline. Herb made sure that the boy saw the gun there, just to let him know that saying no was not in his best interests. He was going to be fucked one way or another.

This boy went easy without any hint of a complaint and Herb had a nasty suspicion that he was a pro. One of the rent boys from Indianapolis that Herb had frequented so regularly over the years before he had found the road and its infinite supply of young bodies with no meaning attached to them. By the time Herb got to him, the boy already had his pants around his ankles and his face pressed into the upholstery. That made things easier, and the fact that the boy looked almost dead, lying there limp and boneless in the back seat, stirred Herb's passions up. He fumbled the condom on, taking his time to admire the boy spread out in front of him, then with a sigh he pressed inside.

The boy grunted, but it was a soft exhalation more than a complaint. Body sounds, not human sounds. Herb could tolerate them much more easily. He took his time in the beginning, gradually learning the intricacies of the body in front of him before leaning forward over the boy in the cramped back seat and hissing into his ear. 'You want to have the best orgasm of your life? I learned about this thing. This trick. You cut off your air until you are ready to blow then you let it all come back. You wanna try it? You want the best fuck you've ever had?'

Whatever answer the boy mumbled into the seat cushions, Herb didn't hear it. He didn't give a damn what the boy said. He slipped his bony fingers around the kid's neck and started to squeeze. Almost immediately the boy started to buck back against him. That could still be interpreted in two ways, so Herb read it as the answer he wanted. He kept on squeezing as the boy struggled less and less. This was the last difficult part. Herb felt the bones in his hands clicking as he held on as tightly as he could. This time he was going to do it. This time he wasn't going to let himself get frightened off. He had been practising for this. He had been dreaming about this. He had been waking up, aching and hard with just this moment seared into his mind. He kept holding on tight until he couldn't feel any more signs of life beneath his fingers. Then he let go and let the sweet body fall forward onto the back seat once more. He didn't move. He didn't even dare to breathe. This was the sweet moment when anything could still go wrong or everything could become perfect. Sometimes the boys in the past had gone this far only for them to come gasping back to life, experiencing some of that rush that Herb had promised them. This time, the boy stayed still. Herb had always hated it the most when they suddenly came back to life, right when everything was about to become perfect.

Herb let his fingers trace over the skeleton laid out before him, hidden under the paper-thin surface of skin and the barely thicker layer of muscles. He pressed down and felt the cool of the night air already starting to seep into the gift of flesh laid out before him. He shuddered, drew himself out of the corpse and then thrust his way back in with an elated yelp. With each movement, the world around him became darker and more distant until there was nothing left except for him and this body. This perfect gift that he had given himself as god of his tiny dark universe. He had eternity to enjoy this little treasure now. All of time from now until this toy was nothing but dry bones to ravish it. All that he had ever wanted was a corpse to play with. A body of his very own. His puerile explorations of birds and animals had all been leading to this. His entire life had been leading to this one perfect moment where he could be left alone with his pleasures.

Hours later, Herb returned to his own body. He was shaking and weak after the exertions of the night. He barely had enough strength to haul the ruined corpse of the boy out and dump it by the roadside. What had once been a living, breathing person was now exactly what Herb had always dreamed. Roadkill, dumped by the side of the road, discarded and forgotten.

It is unknown exactly how many hitchhikers suffered this fate as even the survivors took any knowledge of the experience to their graves. The boys were drifters for the most part. Kids with stable family lives didn't tend to end up hitchhiking down the side of the road in the middle of the night, so most of them went unmissed for a very long time. Eventually, the police began to discover the bodies, but with no real societal pressure to track down the killer of what appeared to be homeless homosexual prostitutes, they were just stacked up for later consideration. Labelled as likely being the work of a serial killer, but not the highest priority task of the day. There were a few witnesses over the years who came forward when the police went to the effort of putting out a call for information, and one of them had seen a man picking up one of the victims from a truck stop on the I-70 one evening. This witness sat down with a police sketch artist and produced a picture that is unmistakably Herb, but the picture was never circulated, and even if it was, who would ever suspect Herb Baumeister, patron of charities and the pillar of the Indianapolis community, of such heinous crimes?

One of the main reasons that the police put so little effort into investigating the string of killings on the I-70 was because of an entirely different set of killings that happened shortly after, during the time when Herb was making his business trips for Sav-A-Lot rather than making door-to-door sales runs. There were several isolated malls and shopping centres dotted along the interstate and some sandy-haired, young-looking white man of Herb's height and build was walking into them a few minutes before closing time, finding an isolated woman in one of the stores, and shooting her with a .22 calibre pistol. Over the course of two months, this man killed five women and one man, who was shot from behind after being mistaken for a woman due to his long hair and slender build. Two more attempts were made shortly afterwards, but everyone survived thanks to the gun jamming. Examination of the ballistics evidence showed that the perpetrator had been using jewellers rouge to try and clear the barrel of the pistol and prevent further jams of this type. Jewellers rouge was used frequently in the thrift store to remove scratches on glass, Bakelite, and acrylics or to polish silver and gold when it came through their door. Herb was known to own a .22 calibre pistol that he took with him on his business trips for protection, keeping it stored in the car's glove compartment. He had attended firing ranges in Indianapolis with many of his Young Republican friends and was rumoured to be a pretty good shot. He was familiar enough with forensics through his friends in the police force to know that taking it into a gun-shop for repairs might create a link between him and these crimes.

While the sexually motivated strangulation of men made perfect sense for the gay and morbid Herb Baumeister, these killings were less logical. The methodology of the crimes was so different that they almost seem like the work of a completely different killer. Indeed, to this day there remains debate about whether or not Herb was responsible for these murders. Evidence that was gathered much later seems to corroborate with the eye-witness accounts that Herb was responsible for these shootings, but the logic behind these particular murders can be more difficult to understand. The killings were supremely impersonal: he walked up to strangers and shot them in the back of the head, a far cry from the extremely intimate murders that he had indulged in so far. We already recognise that Herb disassociated constantly, fragmenting his personality into acceptable and unacceptable personas that he would try to adopt at the appropriate time. We also know that this put a great deal of stress on Herb. Creating situations where he was suicidal when he was not able to integrate the different sides of his psyche, or at least let his dark side out to play. It seems entirely possible then that these impersonal killings represented the other side of his mind, the part that was appalled by the lascivious sexual violence that his dark side indulged in. Killing men in sexual situations satisfied his 'dark side,' so killing women with total detachment seems like the opposing force intended to satisfy the other side. When you consider that Herb placed the blame for everything wrong in his life firmly at the feet of two women—his mother and Julie—these killings start to make a lot more sense. If it wasn't for those women, he would not need to play at heterosexuality, he would not have to pretend that he was a morally upstanding citizen of Indianapolis. In his mind, killing those women would set him free to be who he was always meant to be. But of course, killing his wife or mother were completely repugnant thoughts to the 'good' side of Herb, so he had to find some other outlet for that impulse. By killing these random women, the only women whom Herb was likely to interact with outside of his family, perhaps he sought some sort of revenge on women in general for shaping the world into a place where he could not happily exist by their mere presence. Regardless, it would be many years before these connections came to light.

Lonely Summer

With the success of Sav-A-Lot and his new luxurious lifestyle, you might have expected Herb would be happy, but his internal problems and the loss of his time on the road had been building up to create a considerable amount of anguish. While the store was still highly successful, Herb would not stop pushing to keep on growing the business. He attended auctions constantly and before long the whole house was packed with excess stock that there was no room for in the carefully curated thrift stores. Every room of their house—from the barely used master bedroom to the space around the indoor pool – was packed with goods for sale, shelving units, and mannequins. When the children had friends over to play, they were not allowed inside the house, instead being sent to play in the expansive gardens. Julie had become progressively less happy with Herb's decisions as time went by. The hoarding of goods in their house was just the latest of a long line of odd choices that he had made, overruling her opinions. She kept telling herself that Herb's brilliant long-term planning had brought them this far, but now that she actually had the lifestyle that she always wanted she found that it was buried under mounds of old clothes. It soon became clear that Herb had no intention of slowing down. He began looking at locations in other cities where they might open up new stores, despite the current stores struggling to produce the ridiculously high profit margin that he was demanding from them and no support from within the Children's Bureau for further expansion plans. He was always focusing on the horizon, always driving towards new heights and never pausing to enjoy what he had.

Within the neighbourhood, Herb was known as the pleasant one in the couple. His long-polished manners and constant smiling fooled everyone, while Julie's worsening temper made people wonder why he put up with her. When the neighbourhood children came to play with the Baumeister children they would often encounter Herb out in the gardens. He would bring them out snacks and drinks on the hot days. Meanwhile, Julie was never seen outside the house at all if she could avoid it, and on the few occasions that a child got in and saw the state of their home she was furious, chasing them out and barring her children from playing with that child again. She relished her summer times at Lake Wawasee. She had no particular love for Herb's mother after the frosty reception that she received to the Baumeister family, but getting away from the chaos of the house was a holiday in itself. As was getting away from Herb. The small successes he had experienced were making him egomaniacal. Everything had to be done to his exacting standards, in his way. What she had once seen as strong and manly now seemed like the tantrums of a willful child. For his part, Herb had only ever wanted Julie for the mask of propriety that she brought with her. These long periods of isolation were ideal for him. He rearranged the house in the first few days of each summer to better suit his own unique requirements. Then he set about remodelling himself into the kind of person that he had always wanted to be. The person that he truly believed that he was when nobody else was watching. Part of Herb's growing instability and inability to prioritise properly was an addiction to cocaine. He had come across the substance back when he was involved in the gay scene and now that he had the wealth, he decided to enjoy himself. It amplified all of his worst qualities while smoothing over some of his rough edges. Most importantly it gave him a level of confidence that he had never before experienced, even when he was choking drifters to death while he had sex with them.

Herb had been gradually escalating his violence during his time as a travelling salesman, and he had been dumping bodies wherever he pleased. Now with his expansive estate and plenty of time to himself during the summer months when he banished Julie and the kids from the city he finally had the option to kill in the comfort of his own home. All of the dark fantasies that he had been carefully constructing since puberty were about to become a reality.

With this new plan and his newfound confidence, Herb decided that he needed a new, gregarious persona to go out on the prowl with. Knowing that Herb's grand idea for a thrift shop was called 'Sav-A-Lot' it is hardly surprising that the name he chose for himself was equally inspired. Brian Smart.

Brian Smart did not make a big splash when he first arrived in the gay bars of Indianapolis. Coke and an upbeat attitude went hand in hand, and neither was particularly uncommon in the scene of the early 90s. He kept to himself, for the most part, staying in the background where possible and trying not to cross paths with anyone who had known him in his previous visits. This wasn't particularly hard. The 80s and the AIDS epidemic had taken a heavy toll on the gay community and it was as if an entire generation of potential victims had died off. Herb found himself on the receiving end of some respectful nods simply because of his age and continued survival. He found that this little corner of the world had changed in his absence. The flamboyant drag acts that used to characterise gay life had faded into the background, becoming niche entertainment rather than the focal point of the community. Leather clad S&M fans seemed to have taken their place, along with the tanned and toned musclebound bodies of the next generation. Herb fit in perfectly amongst the sadists and the bitter old queens who had survived an invisible war that Herb hadn't even known was happening in his little middle-class bubble out in suburbia. The younger crowd paid him little mind, entirely self-involved and focused on their own hedonism. The only encounters that Herb had shared with openly gay men of the younger generation had been giving one of them a ride home from one of the gay clubs in Ohio one night after he had too much to drink. It is possible that boy was Herb's first victim—he was found dead the next morning—but the coroner ruled the death to be accidental rather than murder. Once again, in the minds of law enforcement, there were victims and there were those who brought it down upon themselves through their lifestyle, and the police had no interest in helping the latter.

Jeff Alan Jones had just turned 31 years old but he was living on the cusp between the two generations—the one that had been blighted by an almost biblical plague and the young beautiful boys who wanted nothing to do with any trace of their people's history. He still came out on the scene when he could, he couldn't stand to be alone. Even sitting here in the din of the early evening crowd, enduring the thumping bass of what passed for dance music nowadays was better than his empty apartment. He spent almost everything that he made in a week on drinks, but who cared? His bills were paid and he wasn't responsible for anyone but himself. He could save money once he was too old to enjoy himself. There was a glimmer of pity in the eyes of some of the young ones that made him want to run back home with his tail between his legs, but cowardice wouldn't keep his bed warm. He had put up with worse than some sad-eyed little twinks in sweaty t-shirts when it meant he could get some company.

There were few men still out on the prowl who would give Jeff a second glance, so he was as surprised as he was delighted to find 'Brian Smart' staring across the room at him. Once their eyes met Brian bumbled his way through the crowd and offered to buy him a drink with a grin that was probably meant to be friendly but was verging on manic. Still, nobody else seemed to be in too much of a rush to buy Jeff a drink so he politely accepted. They stayed there, pinned to the bar for the rest of the night, gradually drifting their way along to the corner by the toilets where the music was softer and the constant press of distracting young bodies wouldn't get in the way of their conversation. This guy Brian wasn't exactly smooth and he wasn't exactly gorgeous, but what he lacked in positive qualities he more than made up for in interest. He was fascinated with every word that Jeff had to say, quietly coaxing his life story out of him over what seemed to be a never-ending supply of drinks. As the night was drawing to a close and all the pretty young things were pairing off, Jeff turned his doleful gaze over to Brian and was surprised to see a wicked grin on his face. 'You want to get out of here? I've got a place just outside town. The night is still young.'

The night was not still young, not any more than Brian or Jeff were, but in that moment Jeff was feeling young. It might have been the liquor or it might have been the night of solid, undivided attention but he felt like a young man again. The kind of man who would take up an offer from a mysterious stranger. If Jeff was young again, maybe the night was too. He slipped his hand into Brian's and said yes.

They left together, hopped into Brian's car where it was parked by the library and then tore out of Indianapolis so fast that Jeff could barely keep track of where they were going. Outside of the confines of the club, Brian was generous with sharing his coke and before long the two of them were flying through the countryside, giggling about absolutely nothing. Jeff thought that he was an old hand at cocaine, but this new stuff was of a quality he had never been able to afford and his head was spinning before they had even made it up the long winding driveway to Brian's house.

Jeff didn't remember much of anything at all until Brian danced him into some weird dark room, lit up blue from underneath. Even then, he didn't pay much attention because nothing was as exciting as Brian's hands tugging urgently at the buttons of his shirt. The trails of heat that his fingers left on his skin. He opened his eyes and gasped when he realised that they weren't alone in the room. There were a dozen other people down here in the dark all just standing there and watching. Jeff froze. A rush of adrenaline chased the cocaine haze from his brain and he saw the silhouettes all around him. His gut dropped. He had heard stories about gay bashing, about criminals who used some sexy young guy to lure dirty old men like him out into the middle of nowhere so that they could rob him or worse. He was on the lookout for that, they all were—if somebody seemed too good to be true then they probably were. Brian hadn't set off any alarms. Yes, he seemed a bit unhinged, but so did everyone else nowadays. Particularly when they had a little blow in their system. Brian had read just like every other guy his age in that club: lonely.

The other man stopped trying to kiss him, caught a glimpse of the fear on Jeff's face and burst out laughing. Jeff stumbled back and only Brian's tight grasp on the front of his shirt was enough to stop him from tumbling over. Still, Brian's braying laughter went on, echoing around the low-ceilinged room. Jeff tried to push him off, snarling. 'What is so funny?'

Brian's laughter died in the echoing silence. 'You want funny?'

He let Jeff's open shirt go and the man fell backwards into the pool, gulping down a lungful of water. The chlorine burned his lung and he struggled to the surface, his sodden clothes dragging against him. Brian was cackling once more, wheezing and wobbling around until he fell onto one of the deck chairs in the midst of the forest of mannequins.

Jeff struggled to the water's edge and caught onto the stairs, gasping for air. But the moment that he caught his breath it rushed out of him again in wild laughter of his own. The two men cackled away for a good few minutes as Jeff relaxed, letting the water take his weight and just drifting in the dark. The next time that he opened his eyes, Brian was crouched down at the side of the pool with a broad grin on his face. Jeff kicked his feet and drifted closer. Brian wet his lips, looking down at the pale, still body of Jeff in the water. He reached down and brushed his fingers over Jeff's water-chilled skin. 'Want to see something really funny?'

Jeff nodded, anticipation building in his chest. Brian lay down on his front, inches above Jeff's face, his eyes locked on the younger man's lips. Jeff pursed them and waited. Fingers traced over his face, caressing him, bracing against the bones of his chin and driving him beneath the water. To begin with he went under without a struggle. It was funny. A continuation of Brian's mocking of his irrational fear earlier. He could trust Brian. This was just a joke. He felt the air in his lungs begin to sour. He felt his arms begin to flail involuntarily. This was a joke. It was a joke. Brian wouldn't do this. Brian smiled down at him as the chemicals in the water stung his eyes. As he opened his mouth to scream the water came rushing in.

Herb held the man underwater until the last spasmodic twitches stopped. He stood and slowly undressed himself, neatly folding each item and laying it down on the end of the deck chair. He stood there in the darkness with just the gentle splashing of the water to break the silence and he let out a sigh of relief. The hard work was finally over, now he could finally reap the rewards of his labour. He hooked a finger in the guy's trouser leg and dragged him across the surface until he could be hauled out. Herb laughed aloud despite himself. 'Looks like we've got some company tonight boys.'

He stripped the sodden clothes off the body, unwrapping him like a present. The clothes would go into the wash along with the rest of the stuff heading out to the thrift shops this week. By the end of the month, the dead man's trousers would be walking down the street in one half of town, his shirt would be hanging up in another and his socks would be... Herb scowled down at the darned mess of fabric in his hands... they would be going straight into a dumpster somewhere. Herb didn't just sell any old trash in his stores. With all of that done, he pressed his face against the cool flesh of the body's chest and listened carefully for any sign of life. The body's heart lay still in its chest. The body did not make a single sound, except for those soft gurgling sounds that all dead bodies made when you pressed against them. Pressed into them. Herb was giggling again.

This was exactly what he had always wanted. From his very earliest memories, a body of his very own had been his dream. He trailed his fingers lower and gave the dead cock a casual tug. It didn't even stir. He shuddered as he imagined all of the possibilities that this night was going to bring. All of the things that he had always wanted to try but been too pressed for time, or too ashamed to indulge in. Out in the dark places between towns he had chased after this dream. He had let off steam and got the evil twin that lived inside his head under control so that its thoughts stopped bleeding through into his mind, more or less. This was different. He wasn't running away and hiding from who he was—he had brought the darkness in. He was cultivating it in his own home. No longer was he creeping around the fringes of society and picking off the dead weight; he was in the heart of it, choosing his victims not by convenience but by desire. He couldn't remember the man's name but he supposed that it didn't much matter now. Whoever he had been before he took Herb's hand had all been washed away in his chlorinated baptism. Now he was a body. Nothing more than a toy. Herb licked his lips and then he went to work.

Hours later when the sun was already peeking over the tops of the trees, Herb staggered outside with the corpse slung over his shoulders. Out in a clear patch in the orchard, he had built a pyre days ago when he first started hunting. He had stacked up stray branches and dry leaves. All the dead things that he had gathered from around his gardens were there, just waiting to be burnt away to nothing. He placed the dead man on the top of the pile of wood with reverence and no small amount of sadness. He wasn't finished playing with it yet. His spirit was beginning to flag after the endless hours of creative sex that he had inflicted on this body, he was sore and tender in places that he didn't even know could ache. If his lover had suffered, then there had certainly been no complaints. Herb giggled to himself, then sighed, looking down at the bloodied remains—that perfect cold form ruined by his attentions. He just couldn't run the risk of discovery. There were nosy neighbours all about and all it would take was one kid running by a window to ruin his perfect life.

He felt hollow now. He had finally achieved the greatest experience of his life, the thing that he had been fantasising about since he was too young to even understand what sex was. His light side might still have goals to achieve, wealth to hoard and acquisitions to make, but for the darkness that dwelled beneath the surface, the darkness that had always driven him to be the best of the best, it was all over. He sloshed some petrol from a can on top of the body with a little sob. It was over.

It was all over. His life had reached its peak. He might as well toss himself on this fire too because no moment in his life was ever going to compare to what he had done last night. Tears were trickling down his cheeks, intermingling with the smears of blood and crusted on lubricant. Herb had not cried since he was a child. No matter how badly life had gone awry or how frustrated he had become, nothing had been able to get through the barrier of social acceptability that he had constructed around himself.

The go-getting rich-man-in-waiting Herb Baumeister would never have cried—he was a man's man. He liked manly things, like sports and women and success. What did he have to cry about? Herb fell onto his knees in the dirt and fumbled with a box of matches. He snapped first one, then a second before finally grabbing a cluster of them and lighting them together. The flame leapt up, nearly hitting his face and for a moment his eyes snapped open and he saw the body laid out in front of him.

It was a mess, the mouth hung open showing a pair of broken front teeth, a smear of blood and drool ran down its chin, the torso was a mass of dark patches where the blood had pooled and there was an unmistakable carrion stink to the whole thing.

Flashes of memory came back to Herb from his coke-fuelled frenzy. He remembered how the bite mark surrounding one nipple had ended up there. He remembered his whole body shuddering as he sunk into that chill flesh. As the line between his body and the dead body blurred and the darkness of the indoor pool had filled up with a light from inside him. He smiled softly, then his brows drew down as he remembered all of the things that he hadn't done last night. All of the things that he had wanted to try but hadn't had time. All of the ways that he had wanted to use that body that just wouldn't work when he was high as hell and his hands were shaking. This wasn't over. He wasn't done. It wasn't perfect yet. He could still do better. He rose to his feet and casually tossed the matches onto the body. The makeshift pyre caught alight with a woof of displaced air. Herb grinned down into the flames as the features of his toy blackened and crisped away.

This was just like all of the other evil that he had done. It was just to keep the darkness at bay. He wasn't doing it because he liked it. He was doing it because it kept people safe. He was a hero really. Wrestling with the monster inside his skull to keep his kids and his wife away from harm. Not like some of the animals out there who pissed where they ate. He was a good guy and what he had done last night was a good thing. If choking out those rent boys on the side of the road had kept the evil at bay for months at a time, imagine how long last night's festival of carnal delights would keep things settled for.

The Summer of Love

Whatever hope of respite Herb might have been harbouring was not enough to keep him from trawling the gay bars of Indianapolis for more prey in the nights that followed. He eased off on his cocaine use a little as he was quite upset to discover how badly it had impaired his memories of his special night with Jeff Jones. The next time that he killed, he wanted to remember every moment. While he had taken care not to remember Jeff's name, he was profoundly aware of the difference between hunting out on the empty road and choosing victims in his hometown. There was a new element of danger, but there was also an affirmation that this wasn't all just a dream. It was really happening. He was really killing real people. He was brimming over with confidence after his first 'proper' kill and that confidence made him more attractive to his potential victims. He had dawdled through the first half of the summer while Julie and the kids were away without getting enough courage together to hunt, and now he felt like time was running out if he wanted to get another victim in before his opportunity passed. Before too long, this combination led Herb to make his first real mistake. He may not have been addled by drugs when he went after his next victim.

Alan Broussard was running late when he finally found a parking space. Brothers was one of the hottest gay bars in town, and on a Saturday night at the height of summer, it was packed from wall to wall. That spilled out onto the streets, and for every car that Alan recognised as a local's, there was a half dozen belonging to folks from out of town, drawn to the big city lights like moths. They always came pouring in at the weekends—it was easier to endure a whole week of lying about who you were if you got the chance to let yourself out at the weekend. It wasn't like there was a thriving community for people like Alan out in rural Indiana. He had been a late bloomer compared to some of the teenagers that he saw sashaying from their cars into Brothers. It wasn't until his twenties that he knew for certain that his parents' plans for his future didn't quite line up with his own, and they had to have a very awkward conversation. His father seemed to take it harder than his mother, who only seemed put out that there wasn't going to be any grandchildren in her future. Whatever problems his dad had with his only son being gay he had managed to swallow quickly enough that a rift never got a chance to form. Which was lucky really, because god knows he barely had enough time left as it was.

The hair on the back of Alan's neck prickled as eyes in the crowd raked over him. There was a time not so long ago that his eyes would have been raking right back—even now he had to restrain himself a little when a particularly handsome guy strolled by—but Alan was off the market and he had absolutely no intention of ever going back on it if he had any say in the matter. His boyfriend was already in Brothers, probably standing by the bar tapping his foot. It was new enough still that just thinking the word 'boyfriend' gave him a little bit of a rush. He heard a giggle from one of the cars parked right outside the bar. 'Somebody's in love. I saw that smile.'

Alan laughed involuntarily, his grin spreading. The guy in the car was grinning right back at him. 'Oh, I remember that feeling. I hope that man of yours knows how lucky he is.'

Alan just rolled his eyes but the guy in the car was persistent. 'You out for a good time tonight? You and your man? I've got something that could make it even better.'

That was enough to make Alan stop and squint into the shadowed interior of the car. This guy really did not look like a drug dealer. 'Uh. What?'

'I'm not out here trying to sell you a thing. I just want to help share the joy, you know? I see you smiling like that, it makes me want to smile too.' He leaned over and stuck his hand out the window. 'Where are my manners? I'm Brian. Brian Smart.'

With no better plan, Alan shook his hand. 'That's great. I'm Alan. Nice to meet you. Listen. I'm running late as it is, can I catch you later?'

Brian made a hissing noise as Alan tried to draw his hand away. 'Not going to work for me pal. I'm just heading out. Long day, you know? Come on. Hop in and I'll give you a bump and a little bit to take with you for your boyfriend.'

The word sent another shiver through Alan and he couldn't help but smile down at the gormless face of this harmless weirdo. 'You know what? Why not. It's the weekend.'

Brian cackled. 'Hop in, buddy.'

Alan cast a glance up at Brothers and shrugged to himself. He was already late. Another minute or two wasn't going to make a difference. Besides, it was amazing how quickly disappointment that you had shown up a little bit late could turn into delight when you showed up a little bit late with party favours to share. He walked as casually as he could around to the passenger side and then climbed in. The door locks clicked shut and the engine started as Alan got in. 'Hey, what are you doing?'

'You want to do blow in front of the busiest bar in Indianapolis? You got some sort of prison fantasy you're trying to live out?'

They pulled out before Alan had a chance to reply and sped off along the road. 'I'll drop you right where you need to be when you're done. Don't worry so much.'

As if by magic he laid a line of sparkling white powder from a little baggie onto the arm of the car seat. Alan froze for a moment. Everything seemed to be happening too fast, but this guy Brian was still grinning at him like nothing was wrong in the whole world. Maybe if everything was going too fast for Alan he just needed to catch up to speed. He snorted the line and then fell back in his seat, shuddering. 'Holy shit. This is some good stuff.'

'Only the best for you, lover boy.'

Through the chemical haze, Alan heard the screeching of tyres, and he faintly remembered something important. 'You… you can… take me back now.'

'You want me to take you home?'

'Slow. Slow down.'

'Life is too short for driving slow, don't you know?'

'I need to go to Brothers. My boyfriend…'

'Which is it? Your brother's house or your boyfriend's house? This isn't a taxi service. I'm not going to take you all over town.'

Alan sneezed and it felt like his brain had just popped back into his head. 'What the hell is your problem? I need to go back to the bar. My boyfriend is waiting for me.'

Brian sniggered. 'Your boyfriend. Awww. Did he take you to prom? Does he hold your hand? How cute. You are just so fucking adorable. Young love is so beautiful.'

The car swerved from side to side as Brian rambled and Alan had to grab onto the seat to stop himself from being flung around. 'Stop the damn car!'

'Do you want a ride or not?'

Alan screamed, 'Take me back to the bar!'

Brian held up his hands. The wheel wobbled from side to side, unguided by human touch. 'Whoa there. Calm down. We'll be back in just a minute. No need to get upset. It was just a joke. Can't you take a joke?'

Alan's heart was hammering in his chest. He shouldn't have gotten into this car. He shouldn't have taken the blow. He could feel things spiralling out of control and he knew that it was all his fault. It was the drugs. Everything seemed crazy because of the drugs. He closed his eyes and held on as everything spun around him. He could hear the blood rushing through his ears. It was deafening. He opened his eyes again after what felt like only a moment and they were out in suburbia somewhere. 'Where the hell are we? What are you doing?'

Brian had a gun in his lap, palmed out from his jacket pocket while Alan was distracted. He kept it levelled on Alan with one hand while he drove with the other. 'Why are you asking so many questions when you could be using that pretty mouth for so many better things? You really want to make it back to Brothers alive, you are going to have to convince me that you are worth keeping in the world. And the world always needs a good cocksucker, wouldn't you say?'

Alan's confusion washed away in fury. 'I wouldn't touch you if you were the last man on earth.'

Brian started giggling again. 'You know. I always thought that is what a guy like you would say. It is almost a relief to actually hear it. Like the world makes sense again. People have just been saying yes to me for so long that I'd forgotten what it feels like to have someone really spit in your face like that. I should thank you.'

'You can thank me by pulling this car over and letting me out right now.'

This time Alan wasn't letting himself get side-tracked. He was staring into the little black spot at the end of the gun's barrel and letting adrenaline and cocaine buoy him along. 'Let me go and I won't call the cops.'

Brian's giggles turned into a roar of laughter. 'The cops? You think they care about you? You think anyone cares about you? You are nothing. You've got no family. You've got no friends. Nobody will even notice you are missing.'

'What the hell are you talking about?'

Suddenly the laughter dropped out of Brian's voice. 'Just shut the hell up. That is what I am talking about. Just be quiet. Stop moving your mouth. Be still. Be silent.'

There was a long moment of silence and Alan tried to weigh his chances when they suddenly swerved into a driveway. The car slowed just enough that he could take his chance. Alan yanked on the door handle and dove out into the dirt. He landed hard and heavy, completely winding himself as he rolled to the side of the road. He had barely made it up onto his hands and knees, gasping for air, when Brian was on him. He felt the man's weight drop onto his back as if he was expecting to ride him like a horse. He gathered his strength to push Brian off but he was too late. The leather length of Brian's belt was wrapped around his throat and drawing tighter. He hissed in Alan's ear, 'You are spoiling it. Why do they always have to spoil it? I wanted to fuck you as you died. Why did you have to spoil that? You were going to die anyway. What difference did it make to you whether I got what I wanted out of it?'

The world started to turn grey and the little air that was left in Alan's lungs began to burn. If he could just cry for help he was sure somebody out there would hear him. He never got that chance. Brian reared up on his back, hauling on the leather as hard as he could until it was vibrating in his fists like the string of a guitar. The last thing that Alan ever heard was Brian's panting breaths as he strained against that tension.

Herb cast his baleful gaze down the drive. They were too close to the road. Far too close. All it would take was one nosy neighbour taking their damned dog for a walk and everything would fall apart. Alan had collapsed onto his face in the gravel. Herb had felt the tell-tale pop of his airway collapsing. Even if he let go of the leather noose it wouldn't matter now, no air was getting into that body. He used the belt as a handle to drag the body along. He didn't know if he could be bothered dragging a corpse all the way up to the house though—he needed to save his energy for the festivities. He tossed the body into the backseat of the car and just had to hope it wouldn't start leaking. It would be a nightmare to get stains out of that cream upholstery, even if he did have the perfect chemicals to clean leather. Herb parked around the back of the house and hauled his new toy down to the pool. The cool air and the dim lights felt just perfect for what he had in mind, and it was easy to hose off the tiles. Once he was inside he gave the corpse a half-hearted kick, then he strolled over to turn off the camcorder that he had set up on a timer earlier in the evening. There would be no recording of his kill tonight. There would be no reliving every perfect moment that he was going to act out with that beautiful body. He had been too cocky. He had tried to use the tricks that worked on interstate rent boys on some handsome, well put-together local and it had backfired. Herb cursed at himself as he stripped off the body's clothes and wrestled to get his belt detached. It was ruined and misshapen by the struggle. What a waste. The body was damaged around the throat, but not so badly that he couldn't use it later.

Now that he was down here in the dark, his anger and self-loathing started to fade. Mistakes had been made, but the end result was what mattered. And while it would have been nice to kill this pretty boy the way that he liked to kill, and to videotape it for his enjoyment later, there were other nights and other boys. He had this one right here. This perfect body without any of the troubling sounds that it was making before. Herb wet his lips and ran a finger around the darkening band of bruising on the body's neck, letting his finger dip down into the gap between the planes of muscle where the throat had collapsed with a shudder of anticipation. He had always fantasised about playing with perfect corpses, but in reality, there had never been anything quite as satisfying as probing into the ones that were damaged, the ones that were broken and ruined. He could remember the jagged feeling of broken bones under the fur of road kill, almost sharp but not quite pressing through the stale meat. He could almost taste the heady stench of a ruptured bowel. In his dreams, his toys had always been perfect, but in real life, they had always been broken. Herb sniggered to himself. They had to be a little bit broken or they wouldn't really be his.

He had to be the one to break them of course. He wasn't going to take some other man's castoffs. He didn't want toys from the thrift shop. Not for himself. He had never really thought too much about it before. He had always just concentrated on the goal. The toy. Not the ways in which he could make the toy his. He was goal oriented, that was what he had said in every one of those pointless job interviews over the years, and it had blinded him to how much fun getting to the goal could be. He knew that he liked to be inside the boys when they died, but he wondered how much of that was just for convenience sake when their bodies were already so close. He supposed that liking it could have been about the sensations too—there was no feeling quite like a man dying around you. He shook off the memory and turned his attention back to the dead man at his feet. All of these concerns, all of this philosophising, wasn't what mattered right now. All that mattered was his pleasure, and he was going to take everything that this body had to offer.

The second fire was smaller than the first. Just as the pleasure that Herb had taken in his kill was smaller. He may have stumbled earlier in the hunt but he was still refining his techniques. There was less waste from the garden to burn this time so he threw on more fuel. The fire burned hotter with more fuel, so when it came time to rake the bones around they would break up more. There were fewer ashes to cover them up, but the rain washed ash away anyway. Every little improvement added up to an act that was closer to perfection. This time hadn't felt as good, but that was because he had made mistakes. If he could get everything right then his pleasure would surpass the first time. He knew it. He just has to do the same thing that he had done with every other challenge in his life. Grind on it until it was smoothed down into what he wanted it to be. He was going to get it right.

On his next hunt, Herb wasn't so careless. Roger Goodlet was much closer to the perfect victim than the relatively well adjusted and well connected Alan. He was an older man, a fixture of the gay bar scene without ever being one of the stars, and while he had a few close friends his only real connection beyond that was his mother. His father had grown distant as he became an adult. Roger was the family's dirty little secret and there was a lot of quiet resentment at work within the Goodlet household that his mother stayed in touch. Whatever bad feelings were at work in his personal life, they didn't reflect in Roger's personality. He was gregarious and well-liked by everyone who he crossed paths with, and even if his relationships were all quite shallow, they were also universally positive. He had a laundry list of casual friends and even more casual lovers stretching back to his teenage years.

Early in the evening, Roger fell into a conversation with a guy called Brian whom he had seen around a few times before. Brian seemed to know him just as well like they had been circling each other for years without ever coming together. That was how Brian said it. Coming together. It sent a little shiver up Roger's back. The drinks came free and easy on Brian's tab and even though he didn't brag about it, Roger could tell that he was some sort of big shot. He seemed way too calm for their situation like he wasn't nervous at all about where the night was going to lead. Roger had never seen someone that confident before, someone who was so sure of everything that the whole world just lined up with their expectations. That was probably more intoxicating than the booze if he was honest, falling into Brian's wake and bobbing along happily. That kind of cockiness might have been enough to scare him off in his early days of dating, but now it was almost a relief that not everybody his age was a neurotic mess. But more than just being confident, Brian was actually funny, hilarious even. He had a sharp-tongued quip about everyone in the bar, an opinion that was just this side of controversial on every subject and before long Roger felt himself falling into a rhythm with him. Serving up jokes for Brian to punchline. Telling boring stories that everyone else had heard a thousand times and just waiting for Brian to add a twist to make them hilarious. He had a twisted sense of humour, but when the whole world was turned upside down, that was the only kind that made any sense.

When the younger crowd started pouring in the door, followed soon after by the swarm of chicken-hawks about Roger's age, he already had his suspicions about where the evening was going to take them, but even he was surprised when Brian encircled his wrist with his fingers and smirked, 'Let's get out of here.'

'So soon?'

'I've got a lot of plans for you. I need the extra time. And you know us old folks need to have an early bedtime.'

Roger giggled even though the jibe stung. He looked at Brian and thought about it carefully for a long moment. If he was being honest with himself, he had planned to go home with him anyway. It wasn't like it would do any harm to go there a little bit early. 'Who knows, maybe an early night would do me some good.'

Brian laughed and used his grip on Roger's arm to pull him to his feet, leading him against the tide through the crowd and out into the last dying shimmers of daylight. They were both grinning as they walked back to Brian's car. 'You know, I think this is the first time I've ever driven home in the sunshine?'

Roger giggled. 'It is pretty early for me too.'

'But when it is right, it is right, right?'

'Right?'

The drive out of town was more leisurely than Brian's usual mad dash for the safety of home. He stopped at stop signs. He stayed under the speed limit. It seemed almost incongruous to Roger that this zany guy would be so slow and methodical when it came to driving. It was almost like his sudden hurry to get home had turned into something else. Like he was trying to time their arrival.

'Wait a minute, we aren't taking the long way home because you are waiting for your wife to leave or something nasty like that are we? You a married man, Brian?'

'Brian Smart is as single as you are my friend. He is a lone wolf. A prowling tiger... a....'

Roger's laughter drowned him out. 'Alright. Alright. I get the picture.'

'Holy shit, this place is huge.'

Brian wasn't giving him the whole tour but they had swept around the building to park at the back door, giving him a good look at the place. 'Eh, it is just a house. Nothing to get excited about. My place up in Canada where I spend the winters is the real deal though. You wouldn't believe how much that set me back.'

'So do you just sneeze and money falls out?'

Brian giggled. 'I'm sorry, I'm just messing with you. This isn't my house. I just watch it for the owner while he is away on holiday. The look on your face was amazing.'

'You are such a bitch.'

Brian grinned. 'You love it. Now come on, they've got an indoor pool.'

'And I forgot my swimsuit.'

'I'm sure we can work something out.' Brian's grin looked about ready to take the top off of his head.

The pool was lit from underneath and it filled the dark room with strange flickering blue shadows. There were mannequins scattered around the room and Roger politely greeted each one in turn as they passed them. 'You are really weird. You know that?'

'Me? I'm the very picture of a modern civilised gentleman, thank you very much.'

Roger kept laughing as he stripped off his clothes. 'Oh, there is nothing I like more than a little civility.'

Brian had taken off his jacket, but he showed no signs of taking the rest of his clothes off. 'Come sit over here, I want to show you one of the joys of civilisation.'

He pressed Roger down into one of the deck chairs strewn around the place. and before either one of them could get another quip out, Roger felt the same strong fingers from earlier wrapping around him. Brian leaned in close enough that he could feel breath on his skin and worked his hand up and down with painstaking slowness. 'Do you want to have the best orgasm of your life?'

Roger let out a breathless giggle. 'Would anybody say no to that?'

'Have you ever heard of autoerotic asphyxiation?'

'What is that, a punk band?'

Brian laughed. 'It is when you cut off your air until you are just about to... you know, pop. Then you let it all back in and you get the best rush of your life. I've been trying it and I've got to tell you there is nothing like it.'

'I don't know... I don't usually go for any of the freaky stuff...'

Brian's smile softened as his hand jerked a little harder, drawing a ragged breath out of Roger. 'Trust me.'

There was no answer, just the soft grunts that his movements were drawing out of the body beneath him, so Herb reached under the chair and drew out the length of hose that he had prepared. He glanced up just once to see the tiny red dot that told him the camera was recording, then he wrapped the ligature around the body's neck and pulled. This wasn't a desperate struggle like it had been with the last body. This one wasn't resisting. This one wanted to die. Herb had seen it in every line of his body the moment that he walked into the bar. This body was screaming out for release. He didn't want to be a person anymore. He wanted to be liberated from all of his worries and cares, and Herb was happy to oblige. His hand started to move faster. There was no reason that this body's final moments couldn't be happy ones. Maybe he would even experience this mythical orgasm that Herb had been promising his prey since the very first time. If he was quick enough. It seemed clear that he wouldn't be. His face turned red, then purple, then almost black. In the blue light, it looked pitch black like someone had flicked a switch and turned off his head. Herb was pleased that he wasn't going to stay like that. It would have put quite the damper on things later on. He did wonder what would happen to the thing still pulsing in his hand after the final moment passed. Would it stay hard? That had possibilities. He knew that parts would get stiff before they went soft and pliable, was this a way to control that? There were so many possibilities now that he was paying attention to every step of the process. The devil was in the details—that is what he told every one of the Sav-A-Lot staff, particularly when it came to bringing in used goods like this particular toy. You had to put the work in to make things perfect before you could hand them off to be consumed.

    By the time that Herb had started to pay attention to what was in front of him instead of vanishing into his own thoughts, Roger was dead. Herb loosened the hose and pressed one ear against the man's bare chest, listening for the tell-tale rasp of air. There was one long rattling exhalation when the hose was removed, like the air escaping from a balloon, but that was all. Herb pressed in closer, deeper into the still warm embrace of the man he had just murdered, and listened for the beating of his heart. There were gurgling sounds as gasses shifted around. There was a creaking noise from the pressure on his ribs. There was no heartbeat. Herb reluctantly lifted himself off the body and walked up the stairs to mix himself a drink. He was going to let this one cool a little before he did anything else. He was going to wait and see what sort of results that would produce. After all, there was no rush this time, no panic or ticking clock. He had all the time in the world, so just like you would leave a glass of wine to breathe before sipping it, he was going to leave the body to not breathe until he was ready to use it.

He gave it ten minutes, then went down to change the tape in the camcorder and give the still bruise-looking face a prod. The skin felt firmer than it should, swollen with the trapped blood, and when Herb pressed on it, his fingers left imprints. This definitely had some possibilities. Herb carefully undressed himself and then grinned into the camera before all of the details started to blur and darkness descended on every part of the world that didn't contain him and his precious toy.

The fire this time was a little bit larger. He made it down by the creek at the edge of his property. When he swept the bone fragments into the river, it would carry some of them away, doing the scattering for him. Even as drunken as he was on the experiences of the night before he could appreciate that efficiency. The human anatomy course that he had taken in college had begun to bleed through into the next semester's pathology course by the end, and Herb had sat in on a lecture or two, here and there. While he didn't like to think of the sordid details of disposal that he was forced to use, he had sought out the education necessary to make most of these bodies completely unidentifiable. If the worst ever did happen then it was unlikely they would ever be able to pin specific murders on him, not without at least half of a body to work from. Not that anyone was ever going to come looking for them anyway.

That first summer ended far too quickly for Herb's liking. He ran through several different versions of the same technique that he had used to snare Roger Goodlet, with little success. Either his jokes didn't land, he took too much cocaine for confidence, or he simply picked out the wrong victims. The pattern of Herb's successful murders always centred on victim selection. In his main body of murders —the ones revolving around his gratification— Herb picked out gay men who were outsiders. He was careful in screening most of them to ensure that they had no real ties to the community and that they were unlikely to put up much resistance. The fantasies that he could fulfil were always limited by his own physique and capabilities, just as they had been back in school. There, he couldn't be the centre of popularity because he didn't have the athletic body required to participate in sports. He craved muscular macho bodies, both as an ideal for himself and as idealised sexual partners, but his own limitations prevented him from acquiring either. Now that Herb had devised a methodology for capturing and killing that relied on trickery rather than brute force, he may have tried his chances with a few more robust men, but he still feared that they might overpower him physically, or worse, sexually. His fragile ego would not have been able to withstand either of those blows, so instead, he sought out easier prey. For all that he might have tried to justify it to himself as if he were some predator culling the herd of its weakest members, he was ultimately a coward.

Downward Spiral

Herb cut off his attempts to lure another man back with him several days before Julie was due to return home and went through the laborious process of cleaning up anything that he considered to be evidence of his transgressions, although how anyone could notice something out of place in a home like Fox Hollow Farm is a mystery. Herb's hoarding had continued to spiral out of control. Even though much of the day-to-day running of the thrift shop had passed out of his hands, he still went on constant trips to auctions to acquire new stock—all of it surplus to requirements—that he then had to find space for in the family home.

When Julie returned from the placid and tidy condo on the lakefront, it wasn't any of Herb's secrets that drove a wedge between them: it was the ruined state of their once beautiful home. She would have endured any amount of strangeness from Herb if it meant that she got the house and the kids and the money, but Herb was burying all of the good things under heaps of trash. He had always been distant when they were alone together, physically present but emotionally closed off. To begin with, she had thought that he was shy, then that it was some aspect of the mental illness that he had been rushed off to be diagnosed with, but now she was starting to believe that he may just be a cold man. She kept waiting for a glimpse of the softness under his hardened exterior, some glimmer of humanity under his ever-present façade of toxic masculinity, but underneath the surface of Herb, there was nothing but an echoing black void.

The things that had seemed like virtues when they first met had very quickly switched to being vices. He followed her around the house, trying to go through the motions of a normal relationship to the point that she never had a moment's rest except during those blissful moments when he went on a business trip or she went to stay with his mother, who gave a fairly frosty reception herself. Julie's political views had never wavered, but Herb's seemed to come from a place of vicious persecution more than any reasonable conservative viewpoint. He seemed like he wanted the poor to suffer, rather than wanting them to lift themselves up from the gutter. While Julie was disdainful of the more sordid elements of society, Herb seemed to be deeply invested in their misery. When stories about missing and murdered gay men started showing up in the news, he followed the stories like a hawk. Practically salivating as each salacious detail slipped out. Their marriage was strained throughout their successes, so when the business hit a plateau and the money stopped flowing so freely it plunged them into a crisis. Julie wouldn't even speak to Herb most days, and despite her religious upbringing, she was close to filing for divorce by the time that she went back to his mother's condo for the summer.

Herb's winter was cold and unpleasant, more because of his home life than any particularly bad weather. The kids were getting old enough to recognise some of the oddities in their father's character, and on more than one occasion his joking around with them had ended in one of them crying. With his family around him, he was under pressure to act normal at all times, and while he had managed to stumble through the routines of a normal life up until this point, now that his darker impulses had been given free reign, he was finding it harder and harder not to resent every moment that he had to hide his true self. He had come to accept very early in life that nobody else was ever going to love him or care for him, that he was fundamentally different from those around him, and that they would be repulsed the moment that he exposed himself. He became more and more withdrawn at home, and while his business seemed to be spluttering to a halt, Herb couldn't bring himself to care enough about it to do anything. The best that he managed was going in to verbally abuse the staff every few days. This led to morale plummeting, his reputation as a savvy businessman fading, and the gradual decline of Sav-A-Lot. By the time that Julie was ready to leave the city for the next summer, it wasn't even a lie to say that Herb needed to stay behind and tend to the business.

Things were not looking good, and even though Herb was incapable of feeling empathy for others, he could read facial expressions and body language like a seasoned professional. If the money went away, Julie would leave him and take the kids too. He would lose the only shield that he had to protect his alternative lifestyle from the public eye, and once Julie got free of him there was no guarantee that she wouldn't start sharing odd details about him that would destroy his reputation and turn suspicion on him. He had to keep her close. Even as she tormented him with her blatant loathing, he had to keep in her good graces. It was like living with his mother all over again, this woman with far too much power held over him, barely held back from completely destroying his life by only the thinnest barrier of self-deception.

Julie's ability to lie to herself hit its first real test late in the spring, only a week or two before she planned to flee the chaotic mess of their house for the summer once more. Erich had been out playing in the orchard all morning, giving her a few moments of blessed peace. She loved the boy dearly but he always wanted to be the centre of attention and it got a little wearing, particularly when his younger sister seemed to be so easy to handle. The girls had seemed almost painless in comparison, playing happily by themselves. Julie sighed wistfully—boys will be boys. She heard Erich thundering along the gravel path outside, heading for the back door, and she had just long enough to roll her eyes and plaster on her kindly mothering smile before he burst in. He was filthy as usual, but just as Julie was readying herself to send him right back outside to wash, she froze. 'Mommy, look what I found!'

He was holding a human skull.

Julie, usually so quick with her words, so ready to prod her children, or husband, along with a gentle turn of phrase, was speechless. Erich wandered over and put the mud-crusted skull down on the kitchen counter. 'Do you think it is from olden times? Everybody from olden times turned into skeletons. That's what they said in school. Was it the people that lived in this house before us?'

Julie took a step towards the thing on the table and shuddered. 'Where did you find this, Erich?'

'Out in the trees. There are lots of bones there. Maybe a whole person!'

She took a deep breath and then took his muddy hand in her own. 'Show me.'

When Herb got home from work that night the house was unusually quiet. He wandered a little, looking for everyone before he finally came into the kitchen, where Julie was sitting in the dark with bones strewn across the table. 'Would you like to explain this?'

'Didn't you take that anatomy class with me? I think you know what a skeleton is. The head-bone is connected to the—'

'You are not funny. What is it doing in our yard, Herb?'

Herb swallowed back his first snappy reply and sat himself down opposite his wife without a care in the world. She might not be able to read people like him, but if he let any of the tension show then she might suspect a lie. It wouldn't be enough to turn everything upside down, but if she brought the police in then there was no telling how much they would be able to find despite all his best efforts. 'It's in our yard because I buried it there. Because I didn't want the kids to find it, and panic and have this conversation.'

He could hear Julie gritting her teeth. 'Why do you have a skeleton Herb?'

'They really aren't that uncommon. They come up in the auction lots more often than you might think. I avoid buying them because they aren't really a good fit for Sav-A-Lot's clientele, but there are hundreds of them available pretty cheaply if you know where to look. That one happened to belong to my father. He was a doctor, you know. He used to teach at the medical school for a while, then he kept that fella in his office at home. When Mom moved out to the lake I took in a lot of Dad's old stuff so that she wouldn't have to be reminded of him all the time. This guy was sitting in our garage for about six months before I realised that one of the kids was going to go wandering out there and traumatise themselves. Where did you think I got a skeleton from? Did you think I coughed too hard and mine fell out?'

'It's weird, Herb. It's weird that there is a human skeleton buried in our backyard.'

Herb took a risk and got angry. 'What exactly are you trying to say? Huh? What am I being accused of here, that you need to ambush me after I come in from a long day of working my ass off to pay for you to live like this?'

Julie looked shocked. She had seen Herb lambasting staff over the years, even seen him lose his temper with the kids' antics once or twice, but he had never dared to be angry at her before.

'Herb —'

'Don't "Herb" me. What am I being accused of? Do you think I'm running around robbing graves?'

She spluttered, on the defensive. So he went in for the kill. 'Sometimes it feels like you don't even know me. How badly did you scare the kids when you went and pulled all this out of the ground?'

Julie looked utterly defeated. Horrified at what her paranoia had wrought. 'The girls, I didn't let them see anything, but Erich was the one to find it. He saw me gathering them all up.'

Herb hissed, 'Goddammit, Julie. What were you thinking?'

'I didn't say anything to him. I just—'

'You don't need to say anything to them, Julie. They are just kids. They see things and they come up with their own stories to explain everything. You are going to have to sit down and explain all this to him so he doesn't have nightmares.'

She couldn't even mumble a defence. Herb let out a heavy sigh. 'Maybe we should find you some work to do down at the shop. I think that you're getting cabin fever, stuck here with the kids all day. Would you like that?'

'No. I'm sorry, Herb. I just got a scare. That's all.'

After what should have been the cause for alarm, Julie became a stalwart protector of Herb's peaceful vision for family life. She not only readily repeated Herb's lies to the children about the skeleton, she also began coaching them on what they could and could not talk about outside of the house. Where before all attempts had come from a place of propriety, trying to stem the damaging rumours that might have spread about their family, it now came from a genuine and invested effort in maintaining the status quo. While Herb was loathed to do it, he actually cleared out the remaining goods that were stored in the garage so that one of their cars could be parked inside it—evidence that he had been cleaning it out as he had claimed. When presented with this proof that Herb was at least working towards getting their life back in order, Julie quietly stopped the divorce proceedings that she had been putting in motion. Then, with a lighter heart, she took the kids away for their summer vacation, and Herb was free to pursue his passions once more.

Over the course of the winter, all that Herb had to satisfy him were his fantasies, but even as he dreamed he was working to refine his techniques, planning and plotting. Within a day of Julie and the kids' departure, he had everything set up how he wanted it. The coil of hose beneath the deck chair, positioned straight across from the camera on its tripod. The car fuelled up, with the pistol in the glove box in case of emergencies. Enough cocaine to have him buzzing with confidence through the entire summer and still have plenty leftover as bait for the younger ones in the herd. With his perfected methodology and a lot of experimentation planned, Herb went to work.

In quick succession he picked up many different men, spacing them out by around a week and never hunting in the same gay bar twice in a row. He took his time with each one of them, establishing that they would not be missed and that they were receptive to his advances before taking them home. With the whole summer to play in and the relative solitude of his air-conditioned indoor swimming pool, Herb began to experiment more and more with his victims. He was satisfied with the efficiency of his killing, but he switched up the sexual configurations and the timing almost on a whim to see what results he could get. The aftermath was his real focus—the things that he was going to do with the bodies. Not only did he experiment with them sexually in every combination that he could conceive of, but he also experimented with keeping the bodies to see how long decay took to set in, and how long it took him to bore of them. Thankfully the latter seemed to kick in a long time before the former. Burning the remains became a weekly ritual, on which Herb soon settled a single spot to conduct. He would load the ashes into a wheelbarrow and scatter what was left of his victims all around the property, taking care to make sure no more skulls remained uncovered. The exact number of men that he killed in that second summer is uncertain, as most of the remains that have been recovered from Fox Hollow Farm were too damaged for identification. It was certainly many more than the four that we definitely have names for. Richard Hamilton was the earliest, followed by Manuel Resendez, Johnny Bayer, and finally Allan Livingstone. Unfortunately for Herb, while his techniques had been perfected for his latest victims, the mistakes that he made early on were about to come back to haunt him.

The Investigation

Vergil Vandagriff was like a character from detective fiction made flesh. The grey-haired, moustachioed man was a veteran major crimes investigator from Marion County who had retired from the force to pursue a career as a private detective. Unlike in fiction, his 'loose cannon' approach to departmental rules actually made him fairly beloved by the local police force. Indianapolis policy was that you could not report a missing person until 24 hours had elapsed. You then had to wait 30 days for a district detective to search for them before it even reached the missing persons bureau. The whole process was bound up in so much red tape and interdepartmental politics that it was essentially useless. The percentage of missing people that the Indianapolis police actually found was minuscule. Which was why almost every cop would readily hand out Vergil's business card when given the opportunity. Finding missing people became the mainstay of his business.

He was hardly surprised when Alan Broussard's mother approached him in the summer of 1994; it was one of dozens of similar cases that would pass over his desk each month. He wasn't even slightly worried for the safety of Alan given the information that he was given. The man had been in his physical prime, engaged in a lifestyle that was generally shunned, and was prone to bouts of heavy drinking. Vergil fully expected to find him holed up in a Vegas motel room sleeping in a post-orgy puppy pile before the end of the week. Vergil was not familiar with the local gay scene but if he had any hesitation in diving in to pursue his investigation, it certainly didn't show. He walked among the leather daddies and drag queens without raising an eyebrow, as casually as he would stroll down a suburban street. His casual acceptance earned him a lot of trust. Police had generally been the enemies of the gay community since a community had formed, the fascist boot of the oppressive heterosexual world, but as an individual who was clearly devoted to helping one of their own, it was hard to tar Vergil with the same brush. He created a network of contacts across all the official gay nightclubs and bars around Indiana, posting missing persons posters in each one as he passed, and he was making inroads with many of the less official ones when he came across a magazine called Indiana World in one of the bars. It was the local gay lifestyle magazine, printed on paper that most newspapers would turn their nose up at—but it contained a very important story in one of its back pages, about a man named Jeff Jones, who had vanished last summer.

Alarm bells started ringing for Vergil and his worst fears were confirmed when he had one of his many friends in the missing persons bureau pull up Jones' file to discover from his picture that he looked almost exactly the same as Alan. All that Vergil had at this stage were two missing adult men who may have run off together for all that he knew, but his gut was telling him differently. When he ambled into his office he found his secretary, Connie, comforting another older woman with the same mousy brown hair, the mother of Roger Goodlet. By now the story was all too familiar to Vergil, with many of the stories about Roger's habit of drinking too much and trusting too much being a word-for-word repetition of his interviews about Alan Broussard. Combined with the dull dread that he was feeling, it was enough to send Vergil back to his friends among the Indianapolis police with his evidence that there was a serial killer in their midst.

To say that the police were unimpressed with the limited evidence that Vergil had provided would be an understatement, and even if he had been laden with all the proof that was required, the majority of the police department would have considered a serial killer who targeted the gay community to be a vigilante at worst, campaigning against the moral decay of their once fine city. In the whole of Indianapolis, Vergil found only one other person who seemed to give a damn about his missing men—police detective Mary Wilson. Mary's background was in the sex crimes division, where she had put her training in aberrant psychology to good use tracking down rapists and other sexually motivated criminals. She had transferred to the missing persons bureau for two reasons: to give herself a break from the brutality of her earlier work and to try to help get the city's massive missing persons problem under control.

Mary had joined the dots between the strangulations and rapes that were believed to have occurred out on the interstate with the sudden spate of missing gay men and several buried incident reports about injured male prostitutes from the years before. She firmly believed that a single perpetrator was behind all of the violence, but with no support from the rest of the department, she was struggling to make any sort of progress. Vergil put himself at her service, pro bono. While he might have been a private detective now, his blood still ran blue and he still felt like he had a duty of care to the people of Indianapolis—all of the people of Indianapolis, not just the ones who were considered socially acceptable. Working together to canvass the gay bars, they eventually came up with a few scraps of information. Goodlet had been in a bar called Our Place on the evening of his disappearance, and one of his 'bar friends' had seen him getting into a light blue car with Ohio plates. This out-of-state connection seemed to confirm all of Mary's suspicions that they were dealing with the 'I-70 Strangler', but it was ultimately a dead end. Vergil and Mary did everything that they could to pursue the few leads that they had, but their combined investigation ground to a halt by mid-summer. So, like seasoned professionals, they did what was necessary despite their frustration. They set the case aside and waited for new information to present itself. Within a week. It did, in the form of a friend of Roger Goodlet who had a very interesting tale to tell.

Tony Harris had been a close friend of Roger when he was alive. The fact that Roger's mother even knew his name was a testament to that closeness, and the fact that she knew his phone number had even surprised Tony. They weren't lovers, not in the way that the straight parts of the world might have understood it. Just friends who had sex once every few months, almost accidentally. When he came sauntering into Vandagriff's office and began chattering with Connie, Vergil had expected him to be just another one of the endless parade of well-wishers from the gay bars that he had been canvassing. They had been bringing him piecemeal information for weeks, little scraps of the missing men's lives that nobody else could have possibly known, and Vergil had been filing it all away dutifully to create a more thorough profile of each one of them. The ones who didn't bring him those scraps brought him fear instead. Another name to add to the list of potential victims, a regular who hadn't been around for a while, a casual hook-up who had vanished unexpectedly and even a runaway bartender. He gathered all the information that he could, checked for men who matched the victim profile and gave whatever reassurances that he could. Connie buzzed through to his office after only a minute or two. 'Mr Vandagriff, I think that you really need to hear this.'

Sitting in Virgil's office with a coffee in hand and a haunted look on his face, Tony recounted meeting Brian Smart in a bar the previous night, his gut reaction, and his immediate suspicions about the other man. He had seen him staring intently at the missing poster with Roger's face on it and had read more into the distant smile on Brian's face than anyone might have expected. He had allowed himself to be plied with drinks over the course of the evening, playing up his own intoxication and laughing uproariously at every stupid quip that Brian made. When it was getting late he had drunk just enough to give him courage without impairing himself, so when Brian suggested that they go back to his place, Tony had accepted.

What he was attempting would have been difficult even if he wasn't close to pissing himself in fear the whole time. He had to act like he was interested in a man who wasn't only unattractive but actively repulsive. He had to act like he was drunker than he really was, which ran contrary to all of his teenaged training. But worst of all, in between the many layers of deception he had to keep his eyes open and memorise every detail of the evening so that he could recount it all to the police. If he survived. He tried to push that thought out of his mind. Fear was just going to freeze him at the wrong moment and make him slip up. He didn't just have to lie with his words, he had to lie with his body too. When Brian's hands and lips roamed over him in the front seat of the car before they pulled away, he had to pass off the tremor of fear and his thundering heart as excitement. It was easier once they were driving, Brian had to keep his eyes on the road, so Tony could almost relax a little bit. He was trying to come up with a description for the man in his head, but beyond a slightly prominent nose and a lanky build there wasn't really much to say about him. He was almost entirely nondescript. He obviously had money, from the way that he was throwing it around, and the clothes he wore might have been ill fitting but they certainly weren't cheap. Tony had a suspicion that the clothes weren't actually the problem—the body underneath was just so awkward it warped anything that came into contact with it.

There was a moment of silence in the car after Tony had laughed too long at another of Brian's endless jokes, so he tried his luck. 'So where are we headed? You don't seem like a local boy.'

Brian's smile gleamed in the oncoming headlights. 'I'm from Ohio as a matter of fact, just in town for a couple of months to get a house fixed up for the new residents.'

'I was sure I would have spotted a cutie like you if you had been around before.'

Brian's placid smile was starting to remind Tony of an alligator's. 'Well, I've been around a few times before so I guess you didn't spot me.'

Tony forced a chuckle. 'So that is what you do then? You fix up houses?'

'Why, do you need your house fixed up?'

'I rent.'

Brian tilted his head from side to side as he drove, trying to work a kink out of his neck. 'No, I don't fix up houses for a living. I'm just doing it as a favour for some friends. They couldn't be here to get the place pretty for the new people so I offered to do it for them.'

'So where is this amazing house then?'

'You'll see soon enough. Might have to pick your jaw up off the floor when you do. It is gorgeous. Well, it was gorgeous even before I got my hands on it, but I don't like to blow my own trumpet. Toot toot.'

All Tony could muster this time was a smirk. 'So what do you do with yourself?'

'You'll find out soon enough about that too.' He waggled his eyebrows. Tony nearly sprained something trying to keep a smile on his face. Brian glanced over. 'I'm an artist actually. A landscape painter.'

Tony forced himself to flirt, to keep the charade going longer. 'I thought it would be something with your hands.' He felt a little sick.

They had left Indianapolis far behind and were heading into greener pastures. The parts of suburbia that Tony mentally titled 'rich people country'. When they passed by a horse farm Tony started to realise just how far that they had gone while he was trying to pry information out of this guy. Brian slowed the car to turn up a driveway and on the impressive stone wall at the bottom of the driveway, Tony caught a glimpse of a sign, something about 'Farms'. At the top of the driveway loomed a huge Tudor style mansion, unlit and dead in the night sky. Looking like something out of a horror movie.

'Sorry it's a bit spooky. There's no power in the main house yet. Don't worry though, the pool is heated and there are lights down there.'

'A swimming pool too. Wow.'

With the car parked they came in through the garage. It had three cars crammed inside including one antique, and immediately Brian's house sitting lie fell apart. The glimpses of the house that Tony caught in the darkness definitely supported the idea that nobody lived here though. There were boxes of crap stacked up everywhere and sheets tossed over anything that resembled furniture. Brian took hold of his wrist when he saw him looking around and led him down a spiral staircase into a dim blue light.

For the first time since they had met, Tony caught a glimpse of the man behind the façade when they came down into the pool room. There were dozens of contorted mannequins scattered around the room. Through his grip, Brian must have felt his hesitation. 'Oh don't mind these guys, they keep me company when I am working down here. It gets lonely up here in this big house, all alone.'

Tony blew out a held breath. 'Good thing that you've found me then?'

Brian's smile spread wider until it was glimmering like a blade in the dark and his hands slid up to start unbuttoning Tony's shirt. Things were moving too fast. Tony hadn't had time to prepare himself. He could fake his way through a lot as long as his clothes stayed on but he didn't know if he could get his body to do what he needed. Brian's eyes were dancing over him, reading everything on his face and body language, everything that Tony was working so hard to mask. 'Can I get you a drink? Brighten that smile up again?'

'No thanks, I had plenty at the bar and I still want to remember your name by the time that we...'

He trailed off as Brian's face started to darken. Tony's blood ran cold. 'Don't let me stop you though. This is still a party.'

Brian let out a giggle. 'Alright, let me just freshen up a bit. Don't go wandering now.'

The moment that Brian was out of sight, Tony went to work, rushing around the room and searching for any hint of Roger's fate. A weapon, a clue, anything that you might find lying around in a murderer's lair that would prove that he was a murderer. In the little bar that Brian had set up down there, he found drugs hidden away amidst the bottles. He was relieved that he had turned down that drink, but it wasn't evidence, not really. Brian Smart clearly liked to party so having a few party favours lying around was far from surprising. Tony heard the thumping of feet coming down the staircase just a moment before Brian's feet came into sight. It gave him just enough time to slip away from the bar to the poolside before he could be caught.

When Brian came back into the room he was practically vibrating. Tony had seen plenty of coke over the years and it was no surprise that the twitchiness back at the bar had come from a dying buzz. His grin had been bordering on manic before and now it took a dive right over the edge into terrifyingly ecstatic.

'What do you say, pal, you want to take a swim?'

Tony's smile was genuine—that was a perfect excuse to get out of this creep's reach for a moment. He gladly stripped off his clothes and slipped into the pool. He expected Brian to come in after him, but instead, he fetched himself a cocktail, stripped off his own clothes and stood idly by the poolside, watching Tony's naked body as he did lengths of the pool in silence. Tony was frozen with indecision. As long as he stayed in the pool he would be safe, but every length that he swam took a little more of his finite supply of energy. If he was going to fight his way out of this situation, he was going to need all of it. If he was going to have to sleep with Brian to get out of it then he would probably need some energy too. Although a good deal of it would be devoted to imagining that he was anywhere else with anyone else.

When he reached the end of the pool, Brian had made the decision for him—he held out a hand to Tony and with no polite way of refusing, he took it and was hauled up out of the water into the chill air. He led him over to a deck chair and pushed Tony down into it, his expression darkening once more. He leaned in close and in a raspy whisper, he said, 'I learned this really neat trick. If you choke someone while you're having sex it feels really good. You get this rush.' He reached under the chair to draw out a length of hose. His eyes had a strange glazed quality to them like he wasn't seeing Tony at all. 'You should see their face when you do it. Their lips go blue. That is how you know you are doing it right.'

Tony opened his mouth to answer, but Brian had already wrapped the hose around his throat and his dry, shaking hand was already stroking Tony relentlessly, roughly.

Brian bent over him as he worked, getting his face as close as possible without ever closing the distance. Staring as the blood vessels in Tony's eyes darkened. Sneering as his lips turned blue. Brian's face was flushed and he looked even more crazed than before. It took Tony only a moment to realise that this was how Roger had died. How he was going to die if he didn't do something. With the ligature tightening around his neck he had no strength to fight back against his killer. He had barely the wherewithal to do the only thing that might save him. He closed his eyes and stopped moving. For an agonising eternity, Brian continued to work on him, squeezing tighter and jerking his hand despite Tony going limp. Just when darkness was about to swallow him up the crushing pressure around his throat loosened. 'Tony? Tony, are you dead?'

He forced himself to open his eyes, he forced a painful breath past the ring of bruises already blossoming around his throat. Brian's face was cold and blank when Tony opened his eyes, but as he watched the mask of humanity was slipped back on and Brian yelped, 'Jesus Christ. You scared the shit out of me. You know people have died doing that? There have been accidents.'

With his first lung full of air Tony hissed back, 'Was that what happened to Roger Goodlet? An accident? How many more accidents have you had?'

Whatever Tony had expected, it certainly wasn't the return of Brian's goofy grin. 'You've had too much to drink. Why don't we sleep it off and try again later.'

Brian slumped down onto the seat and Tony had to scramble to avoid being pinned underneath him. In a moment, soft snores started to emit from the man. Whatever he had taken earlier in the evening had clearly taken a toll, and perhaps he was hoping to be able to blame everything on the drugs when he woke up. Tony staggered to his clothes and dressed himself as quickly as he could before heading up the stairs in a blind panic. At the top of the stairs, he made a wrong turn in the dark, staggering through the empty dark rooms of the house. In front of the big bay windows in what was clearly meant to be the living room, he stopped to catch his breath. The terrible choking claustrophobia of the underground pool and the confusing maze of a house faded once he could see the stars above him and a clear path down to the street. He gave himself a quick slap to remind himself that he was still alive. He gave himself another to remind himself why he came here. With Brian passed out downstairs, he had the run of the house. He could find whatever proof he needed.

He spent an hour hunting through the rooms of the house, uncovering a house well lived-in underneath the dust sheets and misdirection. There were children's toys and women's clothes in some of the rooms, and while he wouldn't put it past a madman like Brian to have either one of them, his suspicion was that this was a family home, that Brian had been lying from the very beginning. With time running out and no real evidence to take to the police, Tony descended the spiral staircase back into hell. Brian was still sprawled naked and snoring on the chair, his lanky limbs dangling all over the place. Tony swallowed the bile that had reared up in his throat and made a beeline for the other man's clothes. There was no chance in hell that Brian Smart was a real name, and a name was something at least. Something that he could take to the police. Even if they didn't believe anything else they might at least wonder how he had come by that name. They might at least look into it; if Tony got loud enough they might even come and poke around. Maybe professionals would have better luck than him. Maybe they would find something. Anything. He searched through Brian's jacket with no luck. He had just picked up the trousers and felt the tell-tale weight of a wallet and keys inside when Brian hissed. 'Are you robbing me, Tony?'

He had turned his back to the room, he had taken his eyes off of the monster. It was a foolish move, even if it had seemed like the monster was sleeping.

With exaggerated care, he turned back around with a smile plastered on his face. 'I thought you were going to sleep forever. Come on, take me back into town. I've got work tomorrow.'

He threw the trousers onto Brian, who caught them with reflexes that put any suggestion that he was still drugged to bed immediately. He smiled back, coy and calm. 'Sure thing, man. Hey listen, you are a really good sport. You really know how to play around. We should make this a regular thing. What do you say?'

Tony tried to keep his screaming internal. 'Sure. That would be great. But seriously, can we get going?'

Brian drove him back into town in the same blue Buick with Ohio plates that they had arrived in. Cracking jokes and flirting all the way. He made Tony agree to meet him again at the 501

Club at the same time next week, then he tore off down the street too fast for Tony to get a look at his license plates. Tony went to his own car, sank into the driver's seat and tried to gather his thoughts.

He went straight to the police station and told them his story. He was informed that his story was ridiculous, and he was asked to leave before they arrested him for whatever drugs he had ingested. When that failed, he made a visit to the local FBI office where he was scolded for wasting the time of the FBI and sent on his way. Vandagriff's office was his third stop. But it wouldn't be the last. After Virgil had gathered every detail that he could from Tony, he took him directly to meet with Detective Mary Wilson. The only person in the police department who he trusted to deal with the case seriously.

Within an hour, Mary had Tony in the backseat of her car and they were driving around the wealthy neighbourhoods just outside of the city. They pulled up to the gates of dozens of different estates with names ending in 'Farms' but none of them matched Tony's recollections of the evening before. Everything looked so different in the daylight. Frustrated and growing desperate for a lead, Mary despatched plainclothes policemen to watch outside of every known gay bar in the city. Eventually, she returned Tony to the city with a very simple directive. If he or any of his queer friends could get the strangler's plates then she would get him locked up somewhere that he could never do this again.

By next Wednesday, when Tony was meant to meet with Brian again, the plainclothes details had dropped off. The police force did not want to be seen lingering around the kind of clubs that Mary had sent them to and she only had so much clout within the department despite her sterling record. It fell to Vandagriff to assign one of his investigators to the 501 Club, where they watched all night not only for the blue Buick but also for any of the other cars that Tony had described. At dawn, they left empty-handed. Tony had been stood up.

Once again, the police side of the investigation had ground to a halt, and despite Mary's best efforts, she was quickly shuffled along to her next case. If the only people in the world who had cared about Herb's victims had been the police, then he would never have been caught. Luckily, Indianapolis had a safety net the likes of which usually weren't seen outside of film noir. Despite the money that he had been paid to investigate the missing men having been consumed months before, Vergil Vandagriff did not let the case go. He paid for equipment and man-hours out of his own pocket to keep the hunt for the serial killer going. He didn't do this for fame or acclaim because, ultimately, this would lead to neither. Instead, he pursued Herb because it was the right thing to do and because he was the only one capable of doing it.

Vergil was known to use cutting edge technology and modern techniques well beyond the training and budget of the police department in pursuit of his cases, and that attitude of using any tool that was available had spread to all of the people that he employed too. Connie, his secretary, had her own unique set of contacts that she frequently brought to bear on cases that had come to a dead end: hypnotists who could help with the recollection of faded memories and a psychic who would provide her with guidance that she then tried to pass on to the more sceptical Vergil.

Connie had been kind to Tony during his first visit, and with nobody else in the world who really understood what he had gone through, they soon became fast friends, with him making regular visits to the office over the course of the year. He expressed a lot of frustration with himself for being unable to remember the location of the home of 'Brian Smart', so she eventually put him in touch with a psychic from Ohio named Wanda who had listened to the recordings that Vandagriff had made of his interview with Tony.

Wanda was able to recall several details about the house that Tony was later able to confirm, but when it came time to talk to

Tony herself, Wanda was overwrought. 'You must never go back to that house, Tony,' she croaked into the phone. 'I see a man handcuffed to a bed. Tied up and spread-eagled. I see pictures being taken while he is being strangled. His tongue is swollen and purple and hanging out of his mouth. And the eyes. Oh. The eyes. Tony, you must never go back. That is a hell house.'

Tony and Connie were both pretty shaken by the psychic's vision, and while Vergil may not have believed it, the fear that he saw on their faces was enough impetus for him to press on with his investigation. Vergil assigned one of his best men to begin searching through the suburbs for the mysterious mansion.

Bill Hilzley had been a state trooper before his early retirement and he knew the roads and backstreets of the Indianapolis area like the back of his hand. After only a few days of searching, he came upon a home in Westfield with a sign outside that read 'Fox Hollow Farm'. Pushing the legal limits of his job, he drove up past the overgrown front garden to the run-down house and started peering in through the windows, searching for any sign of the swimming pool or even just a whiff of chlorine to confirm his suspicions. After having no luck, he took some pictures of the house and headed back to the office, where Vergil's excitement almost overwhelmed his professional demeanour. He immediately ordered aerial shots of the property taken and showed them to Tony, who couldn't be sure and strongly suspected that the drive had been longer. Vergil contacted the Hamilton County Police department for information about the owners of Fox Hollow Farm and ran into a brick wall. There were no criminals in Hamilton County. That region of Indiana held the highest concentration of wealth in the entire state and as far as the police were concerned, that meant that everyone living there was above suspicion. From public records, Vergil was able to determine that Fox Hollow was owned by the Baumeister family, but with no positive confirmation from Tony, and no help from the local police, all that he could do was to file the information away and send Bill back out on the hunt.

Descent into Chaos

After almost a year, Bill wasn't the only one who was back on the hunt. After the catastrophic failure of his attempted murder of Tony, Herb had been trying to lie low. It had not been going well. With no outlet for his malignant behaviour it was starting to seep out in his daily life, and with no impulse control to speak of, Herb was struggling desperately to keep it under control by self-medicating with copious amounts of whiskey. He knew that Julie was going to leave him if he continued to ruin their home with his hoarding habit, so instead, he transferred all of the goods that he had once littered their mansion with to the Sav-A-Lot stores, packing every available space almost to bursting. Employee turnover skyrocketed and every new worker that he brought in seemed to be less capable and competent than the last, in no small part because they had no training and were working in a space that they frequently referred to as looking like a garbage dump. He became increasingly paranoid as sales slumped, accusing his staff of stealing or of throwing away perfectly good merchandise rather than selling it along. The quality control that had defined the thrift store's success crumbled in the face of the stress, and before long the charity that allowed him to operate in their name were prepared to withdraw their license, effectively ending his business with a single stroke as they technically owned all of the stock. Herb was perpetually drunk, staggering in to work at odd hours to yell at the staff about their slovenly behaviour before storming out again. It was only a matter of time until the charity officially withdrew their support and Sav-A-Lot closed its doors.

Herb still had just enough self-awareness left that he tried to save himself. He understood that when he was killing men, he was successful and since he had stopped all of his faculties had begun to decay. The only way for him to save himself, to save his lifestyle and his marriage and his sanity, was for him to pick up a man from a gay bar and murder him. It was the only rational solution to the problem. So despite his fear of discovery, that Friday night he dressed up as nicely as he could and headed into town. Without a healthy buzz of cocaine or alcohol to buoy him along, he fumbled his first few attempts at flirtation. It was only when he introduced himself to an older man as 'Brian Smart' that he started to get some attention, but it was completely the wrong kind. The guy immediately jumped out of his seat and shouted out to the bartender that this was Brian Smart and suddenly all eyes in the room were on Herb. He didn't know what was going on, but he wasn't hanging around to find out. He ran out of the bar and drove off as quickly as he could, but even so, one of the patrons made it out the door in time to get his license plate number: Tony Harris.

The number was passed to Vergil, who got in touch with Mary immediately. By midday the next day, everything came together. The car was registered to Herb Baumeister, the owner of both the local thrift shop chain and the owner of a property in Hamilton County called Fox Hollow Farm. For Vergil, that was all the information that he needed. He knew without a doubt that Herb Baumeister was their guy. Sadly, Mary and the police department needed more than speculation, so she did the same thing she had done throughout her entire career of hunting perverts and monsters. She went to confront Herb face to face.

After the shock of the night before, Herb had sobered up abruptly, so when morning came around, he actually went into Sav-A-Lot planning to try and whip the place back into shape before slinking off for a liquid lunch. By mid-morning he became aware that there were people outside in the street watching him. He had become acutely attuned to attention over his school years and the subsequent decade of crime. Attention could mean a lot of things, but most of the time it meant the risk of exposure, so his hackles were already up by the time that Mary walked in, waving her badge at him. Herb was stunned into silence for only a moment before smirking as he layered on his own sickly-sweet version of charm. 'And how can I help you today, officer?'

'Detective. Are you Herb Baumeister? Owner of Fox Hollow Farm and a light blue Buick?'

'I most certainly am.'

'What do you know about the attempted murder of Tony Harris?'

'I beg your pardon?'

'You took Tony Harris to your home at Fox Hollow Farm and attempted to strangle him to death.'

'I did not!'

'Johnny Bayer?'

'Excuse me?'

'Are you claiming that you did not know Johnny Bayer prior to his disappearance?'

'Now hold on a second. I've never heard of any of these people.'

'Allan Broussard? Roger Goodlet? Richard Hamilton? None of these names ringing a bell?'

'I don't know what you are speaking about.'

'Steven Hale, Jeff Jones, Michael Kiern, Manuel Resendez?'

'Listen, I think there has been some sort of misunderstanding here.'

'So you are denying any knowledge of these men? You have no idea why they have all been reported missing over the last three years?'

'That is what I keep telling you. I don't know anything about any of that?'

'So you don't frequent gay bars around this city?'

Herb flushed red. 'I am a married man. Not some sick pervert.'

Mary smiled. 'That is a relief to hear. So you won't mind us taking a look around Fox Hollow Farm, just to clear any suspicions about you?'

Somewhere in the midst of the exchange, Herb's almost comical surprise had faded and the cold calculating creature that he was beneath the surface took control.

'Well now, I can't have you traipsing all over my house. I've got kids, I don't want them getting frightened.'

'Have you ever heard that the innocent have nothing to hide, Mr Baumeister?'

'I don't know anything about that either. But I do know that if you are here asking me for permission to search my home then you aren't going to get it and that you don't have enough evidence to get a warrant to search it for yourself.'

'Mr Baumeister, you are sounding very guilty right now. I just came here to give you the opportunity to clear yourself of any suspicion.'

'It seems to me that you came here to besmirch my good name in front of my employees and the people of Indianapolis. If you wanted to help me then you wouldn't have come down here prodding your nose in where it isn't wanted to begin with. Now would you? If you want to communicate with me again, you can do it through my lawyer.'

Mary's professional smile had never faltered, even as Herb transformed before her eyes from a diligent business owner, to a surprised innocent, to a calculating con man. She could smell the guilt rolling off him, even through the stench of mothballs that permeated Sav-A-Lot.

'Thank you for your time, Mr Baumeister.'

'Goodbye, detective,' Herb snarled.

Once Mary was gone, Herb very carefully walked through to his office in the back of the store without any sign of panic. He knew that he was being watched, presumably by the plainclothes cops out on the street. They would be watching for him, making sure he didn't bolt and following him if he tried to destroy any evidence. He realised almost immediately that his conversation with the cops had gone too easily. That woman Mary was like a terrier with something between her teeth and there was no chance in hell she was going to just walk away. She had something else up her sleeve, some other angle of attack. She couldn't get in to search the house unless the owner gave permission. If she forced her way in and found anything the evidence would be tossed out. She was powerless if she wanted to arrest him, bound up by the law in a way that Herb had never been. He froze as the realisation hit him; he wasn't the only owner of Fox Hollow Farm. He scrambled to grab the telephone off the receiver and called Julie. She answered almost immediately—she must have just been hanging around in the kitchen again.

'Baumeister residence.'

'Julie, how are you, sweetheart?'

'Herb? What do you want? Why are you calling in the middle of the day?'

He grit his teeth and let his irritation pass. He and Julie had been drifting even further apart since she had returned last summer, and despite his best efforts to make her house right, his increasingly vile behaviour had driven a wedge between them that he lacked the emotional intelligence to remove.

'Julie, sweetness, I am just calling to give you fair warning. I had the police in here earlier today. They think that somebody might have passed us some stolen goods. Now I have told them that everything is above board but they asked to search the house too. I told them no because I didn't want them upsetting you and the children. So if they get in contact with you, I just need you to tell them the same. If you don't give them permission then they can't come in. Alright, honey?'

'What? The police?'

'It is very simple, Julie. Just tell them that they aren't allowed in.'

'I don't know, Herb, what if you really did buy something that was—'

'Julie, for once in your life I really need you to shut your mouth and listen to me. Here is what we are going to do, Julie. I am going to hang up this phone, and you are going to tell the police that they are not allowed to come tracking mud through our house. You tell them no. Do you understand me, Julie? That is what we are going to do.'

The line was silent for a long moment before Julie let out a quiet sob and said, 'Alright, Herb. Whatever you think is best.'

He slammed down the receiver and cursed himself for skipping his breakfast whiskey and soda.

When Julie answered the door to Mary, there was already a look of tired resignation on her face. She took in the badge with a sigh.

'May I come in and speak with you?'

'You don't have permission to come in. You aren't allowed to search the house. There is nothing illegal here. There is nothing stolen here. Please just leave us alone.'

Mary seemed momentarily taken aback. 'Stolen?'

'Herb already called to warn me about you.'

'Ma'am, I don't care if you have stolen every single piece of furniture in the building. I am here about a series of murders that we believe your husband has committed. We want to search the property for evidence that Herb had been killing people.'

Julie snorted with laughter, but a moment later she realised that there was no joke. 'Herb? Herb wouldn't hurt a fly.'

'So you have never seen anything or found anything that would make you suspicious?'

Panic was already rising in Julie's chest, but still, she shook her head. A good wife was loyal to her husband. No matter what. Mary slipped a card into her hand. 'If you think of anything at all, you can give me a call.'

Mary didn't expect Herb to ever budge—that man was clearly a sociopath, but the wife was another story. She looked like she was already at breaking point before any mention of the murders and you could have read the look of horror on her face when she was asked about her own suspicions from across the street. She was going to break soon and break hard. In less than a week Mary had a screaming Julie on the phone accusing her of ruining her marriage. Herb had continued to spiral into stranger and stranger behaviour since Mary's visit to Sav-A-Lot. He had become almost agoraphobic in his paranoia, constantly checking out of the windows of the house to see if there was anyone down in the street and obsessively pacing. He refused to even go out into the garden and it didn't take long before Julie was past sick of having him lunging out of the shadows every time she walked into a room. In his absence, Sav-A-Lot had lost the backing of the Children's Bureau and was descending into chaos.

Unable to cope with another moment of Herb's antics, Julie asked him to take a trip to visit his mother and try to relax. Seeing an opportunity to flee town without scrutiny, Herb agreed. Julie filed for divorce on the same day that he left. With Herb out of the house, she placed a second call to Mary: Telling her about the skeleton that she had found in the garden and giving the police permission to search the property.

Loose Ends

The police search turned up several compelling pieces of evidence. They discovered the pool surrounded by mannequins just as Tony had described it, but further in they also discovered the hidden camcorder that Herb had used to tape his sessions. There were no videotapes to be found anywhere. But for all that these details confirmed the story of their only living witness—nobody was prepared for what would be found out in the gardens. They started turning up human remains almost immediately. Bones and blackened teeth were strewn across almost every inch of the gardens, diligently raked around by Herb after his bonfires. It took them hardly any time to discover partial remains of a human skull, but it would take a full three days of exploring the Baumeister property before the police believed that they had found all of the bones that had been hidden there. Julie was traumatised beyond all reason listening to the police recounting her husband's terrible crimes. She had to be prompted to collect her kids from school when the time came, and it was only then that she finally broke out of her frozen state. The plan was for Julie to collect her kids and take them down to the station for questioning before they found a hotel to stay in for the night, but just an hour later she came tearing back up the driveway. Mary emerged from her crime scene, confused by the other woman's actions only to catch Julie as she broke down sobbing.

'Herb has taken Erich.'

Rather than dropping Erich off at school in the morning as planned, Herb had taken him along to his mother's condo. Both the old woman and the child were completely unaware of the situation, but Herb knew that holding one of the kids hostage would keep Julie under control until he could get back and formulate a better plan. He contemplated the pistol in his glove box and wondered how easy it would be to kill Julie, just like he had done with those other women. It wasn't like there was anything left for him in Indianapolis. Maybe it was time for him to shed his old name and move on to the next phase of his life. It came as quite the surprise to him when there was a knock on the door and he was confronted by a half-dozen police officers, all eyeing him up like he was a dangerous animal. 'Can I help you?'

'Mr Herbert Baumeister?'

'Yes?'

'I am sorry to inform you that your wife has filed for divorce and has been granted full custody of your children until such time as the proceedings have been completed. We have been asked to come here by the county to collect Erich Baumeister and return him to his mother's care.'

'That bitch.'

'Excuse me, sir?'

'She told me to go and take a holiday so that we could both cool down and work things out and this is how she plans to work things out?'

'Sir, we have a warrant. Please relinquish custody of the child.'

Herb threw up his hands. 'Right. Of course.' He shouted back into the house. 'Erich, pack your bag buddy. You are going back to mom.'

He turned back to the policemen with an exasperated expression. 'I'm sorry. I understand that you are just doing your job.'

'Quite alright, sir. It would come as a shock to anyone.'

Erich was safely retrieved but the local police had not been informed of the full extent of Herb's crimes, to prevent them from trying to make an arrest themselves while evidence was still being gathered. This gave him the window of opportunity that he needed to escape. He told his mother that Julie had filed for divorce and that he had to return to the city to speak to her, then he vanished off the face of the earth.

Mary allowed news of Herb's crimes to break five days later in the hopes of flushing him out of hiding, which was when she received a phone call from his brother Brad. Herb had contacted him and asked for $5000 to be wired to him as a temporary loan since he was on a business trip, stranded in Canada without his wallet.

From there, Herb was only seen alive once more. A Canadian trooper stopped by a bridge and roused a strange man who was sleeping in his car in its shadow, asking him to move along. The man had a few pieces of luggage in his back seat and a cardboard box full of cassette tapes on the passenger seat beside him. From there, Herb drove deeper into Pinery Park near Ontario and settled down once more to write a rambling three-page note. In that note, he blamed his failing marriage, his faltering business and everyone else in his life for his suicide, but even knowing that he would not be alive when anyone read it, Herb was still unwilling to admit to his crimes or his homosexuality. He ate his favourite snack, a peanut butter sandwich. Then he placed his gun against his forehead and pulled the trigger.

The tapes were never found, but Herb had passed by dozens of lakes on his way to his final destination, so it is likely that they will never be recovered. Still, he had left plenty of evidence behind and Julie, Mary, and the Indianapolis police department took their time to work through every piece of it. Collating his receipts and credit card bills from rest-stops around America and matching the dates to not only his most recent crimes but also to the murders on the interstate, the random shootings of women that had occurred, and many more.

Virgil Vandagriff received commendations from the city for his work and returned to his usual routine, but something was still troubling him about the case. He had run out of resources to continue pursuing it himself, but there was one final piece of the puzzle that he was infuriated to have missed. Herb's brother, Richard, died in Texas in the midst of Herb's killing spree, during a time when it was known that Herb wasn't at work in Indianapolis. The evidence was never collected to prove that Herb had visited Richard around the time of his death, but one of the interstates that Herb had haunted for so long led south almost directly to his doorstep. A death in a family is hardly unusual, but the particular manner of Richard's death seemed strangely familiar. He was murdered as he lay in his outdoor hot-tub, asphyxiated with a length of garden hose.

The police had no leads and no suspects.

Conclusion

At a first glance, Herb Baumeister is a classic serial killer, a morbid psychopath who is so fixated on his own pleasure that he commits unspeakable acts of evil in the pursuit of that pleasure. The fine details of his psychology will always escape us because ultimately they are rooted in stranger and darker impulses than most of us can even understand. Would he still have fragmented his personality into light and dark sides if he had not lived in a society that was so overwhelmingly homophobic? There have always been arguments about whether society or biology makes a murderer, and in the case of serial killers, it is almost always the latter. Herb would not have been any less of a murderer if he had lived in a society that was accepting of people like him. His murderous impulses may have presented themselves in a different way, but ultimately his morbid obsession with death, his delight in torture, and his fixation on playing with the corpses of his victims would have driven him to commit the same acts. What is less certain is how long he could have continued committing these atrocities if society, as represented by the Indianapolis Police force, had cared about the lives of his victims. Because they were different, because they were outsiders, the police were happy to let a serial killer continue picking them off.

They were the lesser dead— prostitutes and homosexuals. The sad truth is that if it hadn't been for Vergil Vandagriff and Mary Wilson's personal pursuit of this case at great expense to themselves, then Herb Baumeister would still be out there killing people to this day.

The total death toll of Herb Baumeister's life is still unknown and the list of names of victims provided in this book is by no means complete. The only person who knew the full extent of Herb Baumeister's crimes chose to splatter the contents of his brains across the back seat of a light blue Buick in a forest in Canada rather than risk letting anyone in on his secrets. Many years after the name of Herb Baumeister had faded from local memory, a family moved into Fox Hollow Farm and they found themselves constantly unsettled. Once again, an unsubstantiated supernatural explanation—in this case, a suspicion that the house was haunted—led to further detective work being conducted. They began digging in their garden and immediately started turning up bones. The crime scene investigators at the time had described the garden of Fox Hollow Farm as looking like the site of some ancient natural disaster, with the shattered and charred remains of dead bodies scattered all over the place— with ribs jutting out of the soil like plants and blackened fragments of bone serving as gravel. They had only just scratched the surface. Deeper into the earth there were more bones. Some of them were matched with the partial remains that had been recovered and some of them seemed to be from completely unknown victims. Much of the story of Herb Baumeister's crimes is based on speculation. We have extrapolated from the evidence that we have to construct a narrative of the events, but he could very well have been operating for years longer than our certain evidence supports. Given the sheer volume of men that he killed in only two years of active hunting within the city, how many more might have died if he had been killing for three, or four?

All of this is only accounting for his crimes within Indianapolis. When he was acting as the 'I-70 Strangler', his victims were even easier to overlook. There is no way of knowing how many more he killed than the few that the police discovered. Even those dead boys would have been missed if he had just taken the effort to throw them a little further from the road when he was finished using their broken corpses. Beyond those crimes, how many random shootings might have occurred along the length of the interstates stretching south to Texas and east across the whole continental United States? Herb Baumeister, in no small part due to the fragmentation of his personality at a young age, managed to become not just one, but three separate serial killers, and he was meticulous enough in his planning and methodology that we will never know the total numbers that he has killed under those three guises. It is entirely possible that Herb Baumeister is one of the most prolific serial killers in history, but because of his perpetual cowardice in the face of scrutiny, the world will never know.

YOU THINK YOU KNOW ME

RYAN GREEN

Want More?

Did you enjoy *You Think You Know Me* and want some more True Crime?

YOUR FREE BOOK IS WAITING

From bestselling author Ryan Green

There is a man who is officially classed as **"Britain's most dangerous prisoner"**

The man's name is Robert Maudsley, and his crimes earned him the nickname **"Hannibal the Cannibal"**

This free book is an exploration of his story...

"Ryan brings the horrifying details to life. I can't wait to read more by this author!"

Get a free copy of **Robert Maudsley: Hannibal the Cannibal** when you sign up to join my Reader's Group.

www.ryangreenbooks.com/free-book

Every Review Helps

If you enjoyed the book and have a moment to spare, I would really appreciate a short review on Amazon. Your help in spreading the word is gratefully received and reviews make a huge difference to helping new readers find me. Without reviewers, us self-published authors would have a hard time!

Type in your link below to be taken straight to my book review page.

US   geni.us/YTYKMUS

UK   geni.us//YTYKM UK

Australia   geni.us//YTYKMAUS

Canada   geni.us//YTYKM CA

Thank you! I can't wait to read your thoughts.

About Ryan Green

Ryan Green is a true crime author who lives in Herefordshire, England with his wife, three children, and two dogs. Outside of writing and spending time with his family, Ryan enjoys walking, reading and windsurfing.

Ryan is fascinated with History, Psychology and True Crime. In 2015, he finally started researching and writing his own work and at the end of the year, he released his first book on Britain's most notorious serial killer, Harold Shipman.

He has since written several books on lesser-known subjects, and taken the unique approach of writing from the killer's perspective. He narrates some of the most chilling scenes you'll encounter in the True Crime genre.

You can sign up to Ryan's newsletter to receive a free book, updates, and the latest releases at:

WWW.RYANGREENBOOKS.COM

More Books by Ryan Green

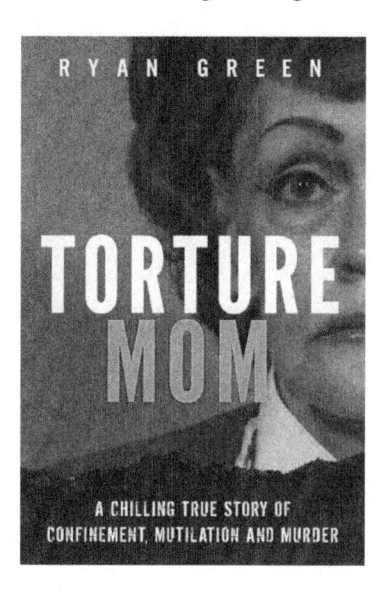

In July 1965, teenagers Sylvia and Jenny Likens were left in the temporary care of Gertrude Baniszewski, a middle-aged single mother and her seven children.

The Baniszewski household was overrun with children. There were few rules and ample freedom. Sadly, the environment created a dangerous hierarchy of social Darwinism where the strong preyed on the weak.

What transpired in the following three months was both riveting and chilling. The case shocked the entire nation and would later be described as "The single worst crime perpetuated against an individual in Indiana's history".

More Books by Ryan Green

On 29th February 2000, John Price took out a restraining order against his girlfriend, Katherine Knight. Later that day, he told his co-workers that she had stabbed him and if he were ever to go missing, it was because Knight had killed him.

The next day, Price didn't show up for work.

A co-worker was sent to check on him. They found a bloody handprint by the front door and they immediately contacted the police. The local police force was not prepared for the chilling scene they were about to encounter.

Price's body was found in a chair, legs crossed, with a bottle of lemonade under his arm. He'd been decapitated and skinned. The "skin-suit" was hanging from a meat hook in the living room and his head was found in the kitchen, in a pot of vegetables that was still warm. There were two plates on the dining table, each had the name of one of Price's children on it.

She was attempting to serve his body parts to his children.

More Books by Ryan Green

In 1902, at the age of 11, Carl Panzram broke into a neighbour's home and stole some apples, a pie, and a revolver. As a frequent troublemaker, the court decided to make an example of him and placed him into the care of the Minnesota State Reform School. During his two-year detention, Carl was repeatedly beaten, tortured, humiliated and raped by the school staff.

At 15-years old, Carl enlisted in the army by lying about his age but his career was short-lived. He was dishonourably discharged for stealing army supplies and was sent to military prison. The brutal prison system sculpted Carl into the man that he would remain for the rest of his life. He hated the whole of mankind and wanted revenge.

When Carl left prison in 1910, he set out to rob, burn, rape and kill as many people as he could, for as long as he could. His campaign of terror could finally begin and nothing could stand in his way.

More Books by Ryan Green

In 1861, the police of a rural French village tore their way into the woodside home of Martin Dumollard. Inside, they found chaos. Paths had been carved through mounds of bloodstained clothing, reaching as high as the ceiling in some places.

The officers assumed that the mysterious maid-robber had killed one woman but failed in his other attempts. Yet, it was becoming sickeningly clear that there was a vast gulf between the crimes they were aware of and the ones that had truly been committed.

Would Dumollard's wife expose his dark secret or was she inextricably linked to the atrocities? Whatever the circumstances, everyone was desperate to discover whether the bloody garments belonged to some of the 648 missing women.

YOU THINK YOU KNOW ME

Free True Crime Audiobook

Sign up to Audible and use your free credit to download this collection of twelve books. If you cancel within 30 days, there's no charge!

WWW.RYANGREENBOOKS.COM/FREE-AUDIOBOOK

"Ryan Green has produced another excellent book and belongs at the top with true crime writers such as M. William Phelps, Gregg Olsen and Ann Rule" –**B.S. Reid**

"Wow! Chilling, shocking and totally riveting! I'm not going to sleep well after listening to this but the narration was fantastic. Crazy story but highly recommend for any true crime lover!" –**Mandy**

"Torture Mom by Ryan Green left me pretty speechless. The fact that it's a true story is just...wow" –**JStep**

"Graphic, upsetting, but superbly read and written" –**Ray C**

WWW.RYANGREENBOOKS.COM/FREE-AUDIOBOOK

Printed in Great Britain
by Amazon